# Minority Depository Institutions: Structure, Performance, and Social Impact

## Introduction and Executive Summary

In the fall of 2011, the Federal Deposit Insurance Corporation (FDIC) announced a Community Banking Initiative focused on understanding the evolution of U.S. community banks over the past 25 years and the challenges and opportunities faced by this segment of the banking industry. Under this initiative, the FDIC hosted roundtable discussions across the country; undertook a review of its examination, rulemaking, and guidance processes; developed a technical assistance video program for bank directors, officers, and employees; and completed the *FDIC Community Banking Study*.[1] In 2013, FDIC Chairman Martin Gruenberg announced that the FDIC would undertake a similar study of minority depository institutions (MDIs) and FDIC-insured community development financial institutions (CDFIs).[2]

Chairman Gruenberg described the important mission of MDIs and FDIC-insured CDFIs by noting, "Minority and CDFI banks play a vital role. Your mission is important. You provide responsible banking services to those who might not otherwise have access to a bank. And, you serve some of the most challenging markets in the country. One way we can contribute to your efforts is by conducting research specifically on MDI and CDFI institutions—to better understand the role they play in our financial system and in our communities."

This study carries out this goal by building on analytical work discussed at the June 2013 Interagency MDI/CDFI Bank Conference, starting with a description of MDIs and FDIC-insured CDFIs and where these institutions are located. The remainder of the study is primarily focused on MDIs, for which the FDIC has historical data, exploring how this segment of the financial services industry has changed over time, how MDIs have performed financially, and the extent to which MDIs have achieved their mission in serving the needs of their community. It is important to note that when discussing CDFIs, the report focuses on the small share of CDFIs that are FDIC-insured, rather than all CDFIs.

### *Defining Minority Depository Institutions and Community Development Financial Institutions*

Minority and community development financial institutions are time-honored institutional forms. Over time, both Congressional and Executive actions have been taken to clearly define these institutional forms. In particular, Congress enacted laws to provide a designation process for MDIs, as well as a certification process for CDFIs. Institutions that meet these definitions may benefit from programs created to support their provision of financial services to underserved consumers and communities.

In relation to more than 6,800 FDIC-insured financial institutions, the number of MDIs and insured institutions that are certified as CDFI banks is quite small. Only 2.6 percent of insured institutions are currently designated as MDIs, while 1.1 percent of insured institutions are certified as CDFIs (in addition to the CDFIs that are not federally insured depository institutions). MDIs carry a number of different minority designations, with half of MDIs designated as Asian or Pacific Islander American (Asian American), followed by a large share of MDIs with a Hispanic American minority status.

A review of financial data indicates that the characteristics of MDI balance sheets generally resemble those of community banks, with a reliance on core deposits to fund loans that are mostly related to residential and commercial real estate, although an increasing percentage of MDIs have specialized in commercial real estate lending over time.

### *The Geography of MDIs and CDFI Banks*

Minority depository institutions are naturally linked to geographic areas that reflect the communities they seek to serve. As a result, most MDIs are headquartered in a handful of the most populous states. In addition, a large majority of the headquarters and branch offices of these institutions are located in large metropolitan areas. Owing to the concentration of MDI headquarters and branch offices in large metro areas, MDIs generally hold a relatively small market share, except in a few large counties such as Los Angeles and Miami-Dade. Minority depository institutions also hold a sizable share of deposits in a number of micropolitan and rural counties. The concentration of MDI offices in a limited number of metropolitan areas is likely due to the

[1] *FDIC Community Banking Study*, December 2012, http://www.fdic.gov/regulations/resources/cbi/study.html.
[2] Interagency MDI/CDFI Bank Conference proceedings—Strategies for Success through Collaboration, June 11, 2013, http://www.fdic.gov/regulations/resources/minority/events/interagency2013/agenda2.html.

relatively small geographic footprint of MDIs, with most locating all of their banking offices in three counties or less. In addition, with the exception of several large Hispanic American MDIs, most MDIs have a small number of offices.

FDIC-insured institutions that are certified as CDFIs, but are not MDIs, tend to be concentrated in Mississippi, Illinois, and California, with more than half of their total banking offices in Mississippi alone. Finally, unlike MDIs, only about half of these FDIC-insured CDFIs are located in metropolitan areas.

*Structural Change Among MDIs*

Like other types of banks, the MDI banking segment has experienced significant structural change over time. The number of MDI charters has fluctuated, owing to a number of factors, including institutions being newly designated as MDIs, existing MDIs being acquired by other institutions, failing MDIs, and the chartering of new MDIs. Compared with the industry overall, and especially community banks, MDIs have experienced a greater degree of structural volatility, with relatively few MDIs operating continuously throughout our 2001–2013 study period. The composition of the MDI segment has also changed over time, with the share of Asian American MDIs increasing, and the share of African American MDIs declining.

*Financial Performance of MDIs*

The wide size variation among MDIs, in addition to the significant amount of structural change in this segment, makes long-term group comparisons of MDI performance difficult. Nonetheless, MDIs appear to underperform non-MDI institutions in terms of standard industry measures of financial performance such as pretax return on assets. MDIs were found to perform much like community banks with regard to net interest income and noninterest income, but generally experienced higher expenses related to problem loans, as well as higher overhead expenses. Smaller MDIs, especially, were found to have much higher noninterest expenses compared with larger MDIs and community banks. In addition, smaller MDIs also were found to be less efficient than both midsize and larger MDIs, as well as non-MDI community and noncommunity banks. Several factors may contribute to these differences in performance, including the concentration of MDIs in metropolitan areas and the relatively young age of MDIs.

*Social Impact of MDIs*

Financial performance is not the only bottom line for MDIs. As noted in the FDIC policy statement regarding minority depository institutions, these organizations often promote the economic viability of minority and underserved communities, namely populations that are underserved by mainstream financial institutions. The study finds that MDIs have much to show for their efforts in reaching these populations. Compared with community banks, the markets served by MDI offices include a higher share of population living in low- or moderate-income (LMI) census tracts, as well as a higher share of minority populations. In addition, among institutions that reported data under the Home Mortgage Disclosure Act (HMDA), MDIs originated a larger share of their mortgages to borrowers who live in LMI census tracts and to minority borrowers than did non-MDI community banks. These findings indicate a significant degree of success by MDIs in serving the purpose that this segment of the banking industry was intended to achieve.

## Section 1. Defining Minority Depository and Community Development Financial Institutions

### MDIs

Minority depository institutions (MDIs) are a time-honored institutional form, with the earliest minority-owned banks dating back as far as 1866.[3] Yet, over time, there has been a growing recognition that more must be done to meet the financial needs of minority communities. Among many responsibilities, the FDIC has long played an important role in implementing measures to expand access to mainstream banking products and services.

There has been a series of legislative and regulatory actions designed to promote access to financial services on the part of underserved populations. Beginning in the 1960s, Congress enacted a number of consumer protection laws, including the Consumer Credit Protection Act of 1968 and the Equal Credit Opportunity Act of 1974. Congress also enacted laws designed to ensure that financial institutions serve all segments of their local communities. One of these laws, the Community Reinvestment Act (CRA) of 1977, "is intended to encourage depository institutions to help meet the credit and development needs of their

[3] See Douglas A. Price, "Minority-Owned Banks: History and Trends," Economic Commentary, Federal Reserve Bank of Cleveland, 1991, http://www.clevelandfed.org/research/commentary/1990/0701.pdf.

communities, especially the needs of low- and moderate-income neighborhoods or persons, small businesses, and small farms."[4]

In addition to legislative actions, various administrations have issued executive orders that provided federal assistance to institutions that serve minority communities. As a result of two executive orders issued in 1969 and 1971, the Commerce and Treasury Departments established the Minority Bank Deposit Program. Financial institutions that participated in this program were recognized as minority banks, and private and public sector organizations were encouraged to obtain services from these institutions.

After turmoil in the financial services industry in the 1980s and early 1990s resulted in the failure of hundreds of banks and savings institutions, including some minority banks, Congress enacted the Financial Institution Reform, Recovery, and Enforcement Act (FIRREA) of 1989. FIRREA established several important goals with respect to MDIs, including to preserve the number of minority depository institutions, preserve the minority character in cases of merger or acquisition, provide technical assistance to prevent insolvency of institutions not now insolvent, promote and encourage creation of new minority depository institutions, and provide for training, technical assistance, and education programs.

With the enactment of FIRREA, the MDI designation also became somewhat more structured. FIRREA defines an MDI as "any depository institution where 51 percent or more of the stock is owned by one or more socially and economically disadvantaged individuals." The FDIC further interpreted FIRREA's definition in its 2002 Policy Statement on MDIs not only to include federally insured depository institutions where 51 percent or more of the voting stock is owned by minority individuals, but to also allow insured depository institutions to choose MDI status if a majority of the Board of Directors is minority individuals *and* the community that the institution serves is predominantly minority.[5] As noted in the policy statement, institutions that are not already identified as minority depository institutions can request to be designated as such by certifying that they meet the above definition.

Although seeking designation as a minority depository institution is voluntary, because of the goals established in FIRREA, MDIs may benefit from technical assistance, training, and educational programs provided by the banking regulatory agencies that are unavailable to other insured depository institutions. In addition, under the Community Reinvestment Act (CRA), non-MDI financial institutions may be encouraged to provide support to MDIs to meet the requirements of the act with respect to the lending, investment, and service tests. As noted in Part 345 of the FDIC's rule implementing CRA, when assessing the CRA performance of a bank, the FDIC considers as a factor capital investment, loan participation, and other ventures undertaken by the bank in cooperation with minority- and women-owned financial institutions and low-income credit unions. Such activities must help meet the credit needs of local communities in which the minority- and women-owned financial institutions and low-income credit unions are chartered. However, to be considered, such activities do *not* need to also benefit the bank's assessment area(s) or the broader statewide or regional area that includes the bank's assessment area(s).[6]

## CDFIs

Community development financial institutions were defined by congressional action under the 1994 Riegle Community Development and Regulatory Improvement Act. Whereas MDIs are, by definition, insured depository institutions, CDFIs may take on any number of different institutional forms as long as their primary mission involves supporting economic growth through investments that promote the long-term economic and social viability of a defined investment area or targeted population.[7] For example, a certification process managed by the U.S. Department of the Treasury's Community Development Financial Institutions Fund classifies CDFIs as those specialized financial institutions that work in market niches underserved by traditional financial institutions. CDFIs include both regulated institutions such as banks and credit unions, and nonregulated institutions such as loan and venture capital funds. (For additional information on CDFIs, see inset box.)

As a result of these overlapping designations, an insured depository institution may become certified as a CDFI

[4] Kenneth Spong, Banking Regulation, Federal Reserve Bank of Kansas City, 2000.

[5] FDIC Policy Statement Regarding Minority Depository Institutions, 2002, http://www.fdic.gov/regulations/resources/minority/sop5-only.pdf.

[6] 12 CFR § 345.21(f) [60 FR 22201, May 4, 1995, as amended at 75 FR 61045, Oct. 4, 2010].

[7] Riegle Community Development and Regulatory Improvement Act of 1994, Title 1, Section 103.

## *Community Development Financial Institutions*

Under Title 1 of the Riegle Community Development and Regulatory Improvement Act of 1994, Congress established community development financial institutions (CDFIs) and the CDFI Fund. Under the act, a CDFI is defined as an entity that has a primary mission of promoting community development; serves an investment area or targeted population; provides development services in conjunction with equity investments or loans, directly or through a subsidiary or affiliate; maintains, through representation on its governing board or otherwise, accountability to residents of its investment area or targeted population; and is not an agency or instrumentality of the United States, or of any state or political subdivision of a state.

Section 102 of the act states that Congress finds that:

1. Many of the Nation's urban, rural, and Native American communities face critical social and economic problems arising in part from the lack of economic growth, people living in poverty, and the lack of employment and other opportunities;
2. The restoration and maintenance of the economies of these communities will require coordinated development strategies, intensive supportive services, and increased access to equity investments and loans for development activities, including investment in businesses, housing, commercial real estate, human development, and other activities that promote the long-term economic and social viability of the community; and
3. Community development financial institutions have proven their ability to identify and respond to community needs for equity investments, loans, and development services.

Section 102 also states that the purpose of the act is to create a Community Development Financial Institutions Fund to promote economic revitalization and community development through investment in and assistance to community development financial institutions, including enhancing their liquidity.

CDFI certification is a designation conferred by the CDFI Fund and is a requirement for accessing financial and technical award assistance through a wide range of programs, including:

- **CDFI Program:** Provides Financial Assistance and Technical Assistance awards to certified and emerging CDFIs to sustain and expand their services and to build their technical capacity.
- **Native Initiatives:** Includes the Native American CDFI Assistance Program, which provides Financial Assistance and Technical Assistance awards to CDFIs serving Native American communities to sustain and expand their services and to build their technical capacity, and training opportunities for native CDFIs as part of the CDFI Fund's Capacity Building Initiative.
- **New Markets Tax Credit Program:** Provides tax allocation authority to certified community development entities (CDEs), enabling investors to claim tax credits against their federal income taxes. The CDEs in turn use the capital raised to make investments in low-income communities.
- **Capacity Building Initiative:** Provides organizations certified as CDFIs or trying to become CDFIs with access to free seminars, market research and analysis, tools, and one-on-one training to help develop, diversify, and grow.
- **CDFI Bond Guarantee Program:** Guarantees the full amount of notes or bonds issued to support CDFI banks that make investments for eligible community or economic development purposes. These bonds or notes support CDFI bank lending and investment by providing a source of long-term, patient capital.

In addition, any FDIC-insured depository institution, regardless of whether it is certified as a CDFI, may participate in the CDFI Fund's Bank Enterprise Award (BEA Award) program if they pursue qualified activities in economically distressed communities.

For more information on certified CDFI banks, including eligibility requirements, please visit www.CDFIfund.gov.

Chart 1.1

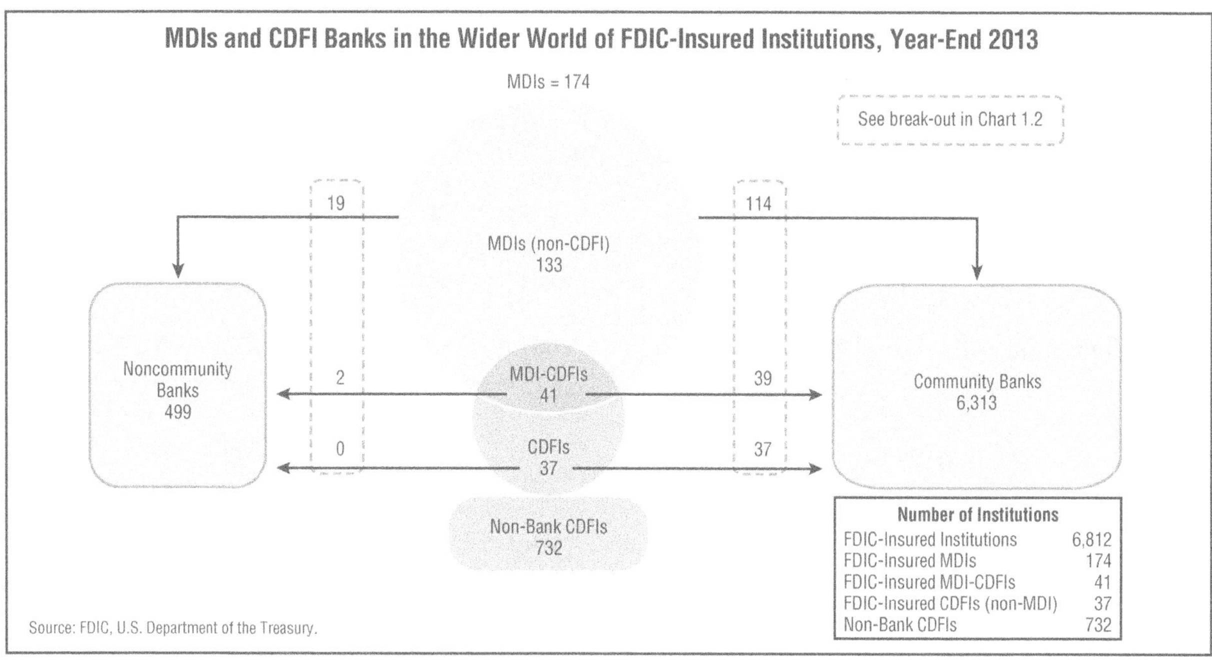


Chart 1.2

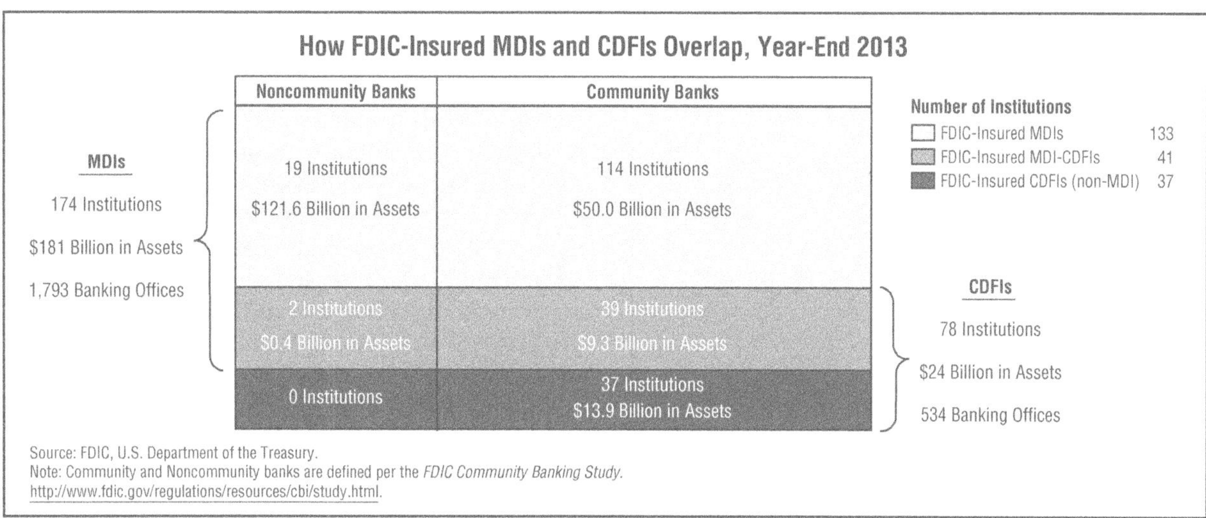


without also being designated an MDI. Similarly, not all MDIs are also certified as CDFIs, although some are certified as both.

## MDIs and CDFI Banks in Context

When considered in the context of all FDIC-insured institutions, MDIs and FDIC-insured CDFIs have a number of similarities to the much larger industry segment commonly referred to as community banks. Among the 6,812 FDIC-insured institutions that reported at year-end 2013, some 6,313, or 93 percent, met the definition of a community bank as outlined in the 2012 *FDIC Community Banking Study* (see Chart 1.1). The remaining 499 FDIC-insured institutions are referred to as noncommunity banks. By way of comparison, some 88 percent of MDIs and 97 percent of FDIC-insured CDFIs also met the community bank definition at year-end 2013.

A closer examination of these entities reveals that the number of MDIs and FDIC-insured CDFIs is quite small compared with the universe of FDIC-insured institutions (see Chart 1.2). As of year-end 2013, 174 insured institutions, with assets totaling $181 billion, were designated by the FDIC as MDIs, equaling 2.6 percent of the 6,812 insured institutions. The number of insured institutions certified as CDFIs is even smaller, totaling just 78, or 1.1 percent of all insured institutions, at year-end 2013. Of these 78 CDFI banks, 41 were also designated as MDIs. While the number of insured institutions that are certified as CDFIs is relatively small, there were more than 700 CDFIs that were not insured institutions.

## Geography and Demographics of MDIs

For reasons of data availability, the remainder of this study focuses primarily on the 174 FDIC-insured institutions designated as MDIs. By limiting the study in this fashion, we are able to identify MDI charters going back to year-end 2001, which results in a study period that encompasses 13 years.

During the study period, the number of MDIs increased from 164 to 174 and their assets more than doubled, from $83 billion to $181 billion. While there are 22 MDIs with assets greater than $1 billion, most MDIs are relatively small. The median MDI held $198 million in total assets at year-end 2013, compared with $159 million in total assets at the median community bank.

In addition to their relatively small size, MDIs also tend to be younger institutions than non-MDIs. At year-end 2013, the median age of an MDI charter was 28 years, compared with 90 years for community banks (see Chart 1.3). Nearly one in five community bank charters were established before 1900, compared with only two of the 174 MDI charters that reported in 2013.

Most MDIs are owned or managed by individuals from a specific minority group. Thus MDIs may be designated as having a minority status of Asian or Pacific Islander American (Asian American), Black or African American (African American), Hispanic American, Native American or Alaskan Native American (Native American), or Multi-Racial American (Multi-Racial). Half of all MDIs at year-end 2013 were designated as serving Asian American communities (see Chart 1.4). Another 22 percent were designated as Hispanic American, with 5 Hispanic American MDIs located in Puerto Rico; 16 percent served African American communities; and 10 percent were serving the Native American community. Only two institutions were designated as Multi-Racial MDIs.

Chart 1.3

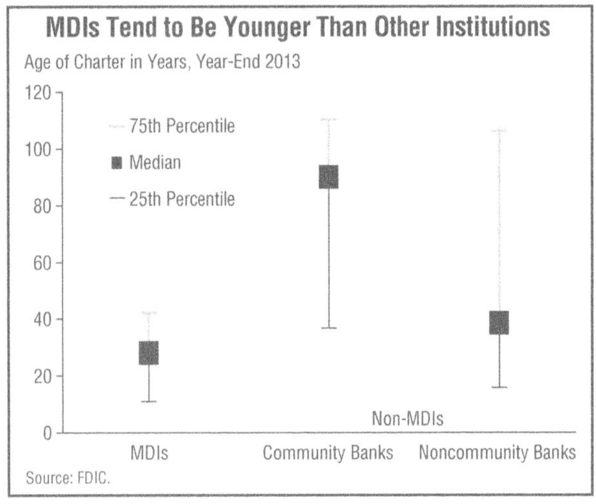


Chart 1.4

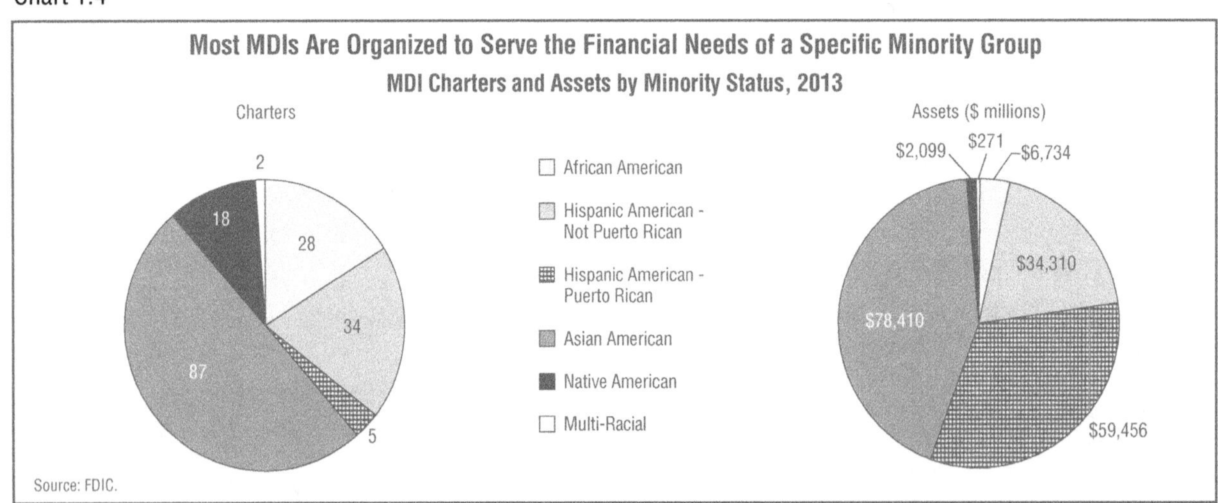

Table 1.1

| The MDI Liability Structure Is Mostly Built Around Core Deposits | | | | | | |
|---|---|---|---|---|---|---|
| December 31, 2013 | MDIs | | Non-MDIs | | | |
| | | | Community Banks | | Noncommunity Banks | |
| Liability | Dollars in Billions | Percent of Assets | Dollars in Billions | Percent of Assets | Dollars in Billions | Percent of Assets |
| Core Deposits | $130 | 71% | $1,583 | 80% | $7,319 | 58% |
| Other Deposits | $13 | 7% | $52 | 3% | $2,095 | 17% |
| Short-Term Borrowings[a] | $6 | 3% | $38 | 2% | $683 | 5% |
| Long-Term Borrowings[b] | $3 | 2% | $48 | 2% | $279 | 2% |
| Other Liabilities | $8 | 4% | $44 | 2% | $768 | 6% |
| Equity Capital | $22 | 12% | $212 | 11% | $1,410 | 11% |
| **Total Liabilities and Equity Capital** | **$181** | **100%** | **$1,977** | **100%** | **$12,553** | **100%** |

Source: FDIC. Amounts and percentages may not total due to rounding.

[a] Includes borrowings with a remaining maturity or time to next repricing of one year or less.

[b] Includes borrowings with a remaining maturity or time to next repricing of more than one year.

The largest share of MDI assets are held by Hispanic American MDIs, which held 52 percent of MDI assets at year-end 2013. Among these institutions, five Hispanic American MDIs headquartered in Puerto Rico held $59.5 billion in assets—nearly a third of all MDI assets. An additional 43 percent of MDI assets were held by Asian American MDIs. And while African American MDIs make up 16 percent of MDI charters, they held less than 4 percent of MDI assets at year-end 2013.

## Balance Sheet Characteristics

As most MDI-designated institutions also meet the definition of a community bank as described in the *FDIC Community Banking Study*, their balance sheet characteristics generally resemble those of other community banks. Like community banks, MDIs have a liability structure primarily built on core deposits.[8] MDIs fund 71 percent of their portfolios through core deposits, a ratio that is slightly lower than the community bank core deposit ratio of 80 percent, but higher than the noncommunity bank ratio of 58 percent (see Table 1.1).

The asset portfolio of MDIs also resembles the community bank portfolio (see Table 1.2). Nearly half of MDI assets consist of loans secured by residential and commercial real estate, compared with 47 percent for community banks and 23 percent for noncommunity banks. Like community banks, MDIs also hold a disproportionate percentage of small loans to businesses and farms.[9] MDIs held almost $15 billion in loans to small business in 2013, equaling 2.2 percent of the industry total, despite holding only a 1.2 percent share of industry assets.

### *Lending Specialty Group*

MDI institutions not only have a higher share of total loans secured by real estate, but also exhibit higher concentrations in loans secured by commercial real estate (CRE) lending than community or noncommunity banks. This is especially apparent when identifying CRE specialists according to the lending specialty definitions used in the *FDIC Community Banking Study*. At year-end 2013, 58 percent of MDIs met the definition of a commercial real estate specialist, compared with 22 percent of community banks (see Chart 1.5).[10] By

[8] Core deposits are defined as domestic deposits less brokered deposits. Historically, core deposits have been defined for analytical and examination purposes as the sum of demand deposits, all NOW and automatic transfer service accounts, money market deposit accounts, other savings deposits, and time deposits under $100,000. On March 31, 2011, this definition was revised to reflect the permanent increase in FDIC deposit insurance coverage from $100,000 to $250,000 and to exclude insured brokered deposits from core deposits. The definition used in the study provides consistency over time, since core deposits as defined before March 31, 2011, included some brokered deposits.

[9] Small commercial and industrial loans and small loans secured by nonfarm, nonresidential properties consist of loans with an original loan amount of less than $1 million, whereas small farmland loans and agricultural production loans have original loan amounts of less than $500,000.

[10] Using the definitions in the *FDIC Community Banking Study*, CRE specialists are defined as institutions holding construction and development (C&D) loans greater than 10 percent of assets or total CRE loans (C&D, multifamily, and secured by other commercial properties) greater than 30 percent of total assets, while not meeting any other single-specialist definition.

Table 1.2

**MDI Asset Portfolios Resemble Those of Community Banks**

| December 31, 2013 | MDIs | | Non-MDIs | | | |
|---|---|---|---|---|---|---|
| | | | Community Banks | | Noncommunity Banks | |
| Loan or Asset Category | Dollars in Billions | Percent of Assets | Dollars in Billions | Percent of Assets | Dollars in Billions | Percent of Assets |
| Mortgage Loans[a] | $31 | 17% | $392 | 20% | $1,916 | 15% |
| Consumer Loans | $9 | 5% | $53 | 3% | $1,291 | 10% |
| Commercial Real Estate (CRE) Loans[b] | $59 | 32% | $526 | 27% | $998 | 8% |
| Construction and Development (C&D) Loans | $5 | 3% | $76 | 4% | $129 | 1% |
| Commercial and Industrial (C&I) Loans | $20 | 11% | $177 | 9% | $1,402 | 11% |
| Agricultural Loans[c] | $1 | 0% | $98 | 5% | $50 | 0% |
| Other Loans and Leases | $6 | 3% | $10 | 0% | $753 | 6% |
| Less: Loan Loss Provisions and Unearned Income | $1 | 1% | $3 | 0% | $30 | 0% |
| Net Loans and Leases | $124 | 68% | $1,253 | 63% | $6,381 | 51% |
| Securities | $28 | 16% | $455 | 23% | $2,518 | 20% |
| Other Assets | $29 | 16% | $268 | 14% | $3,666 | 29% |
| **Total Assets** | **$181** | **100%** | **$1,977** | **100%** | **$12,565** | **100%** |

Source: FDIC. Amounts and percentages may not total due to rounding.

[a] Mortgage loans include home equity lines of credit, junior liens, and other loans secured by residential real estate.

[b] CRE loans include construction and development (C&D) loans, loans secured by multifamily properties, and loans secured by nonfarm nonresidential real estate.

[c] Agricultural loans include production loans and loans secured by farm real estate.

Chart 1.5

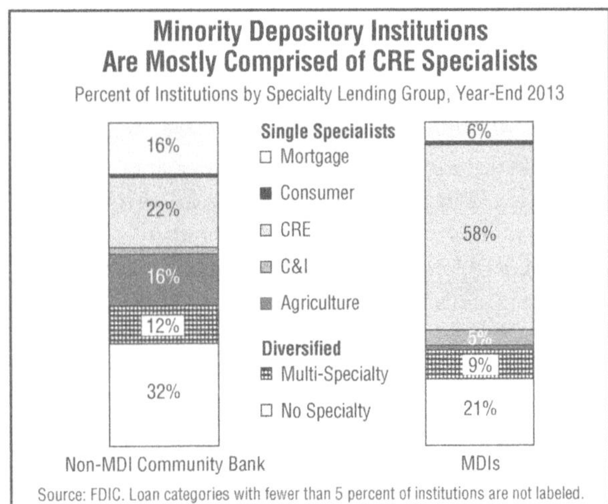

Source: FDIC. Loan categories with fewer than 5 percent of institutions are not labeled.

contrast, fewer than 10 percent of MDIs were categorized as mortgage, commercial and industrial (C&I), or multi-specialty, while 21 percent of MDIs were categorized as diversified nonspecialists.

Over the past decade, MDIs have migrated to the CRE specialty group from other lending groups. A number of MDIs changed their lending strategy during this period from a focus on mortgage or C&I lending to specialize in CRE lending. The bulk of this shift came from MDIs that previously had a more diversified portfolio and met none of the lending specialty criteria. In 2002, 31 percent of MDIs had no lending specialty. By 2013, this number had fallen to 21 percent.

Among minority status groups, Asian American MDIs had the highest concentration of CRE specialists in 2013 at 74 percent. However, more than half of all African American MDIs were also CRE specialists in 2013.

Although a relatively large share of MDIs have a CRE specialization, it is worth noting that not all CRE loans bear the same risk. The risk profile of CRE loans may vary widely based on the property and occupancy type of the collateral. For example, CRE loans may consist of loans that finance construction and development projects, are secured by multifamily properties, or are secured by so-called nonfarm nonresidential properties. Chart 1.6 shows that of the total CRE loans held by MDIs in 2013, more than three-fourths were loans secured by nonfarm, nonresidential properties. And nearly 30 percent of all CRE loans were secured by owner-occupied commercial properties. In many cases, these loans closely resemble C&I loans, where real estate collateral has been attached in an abundance of

Chart 1.6

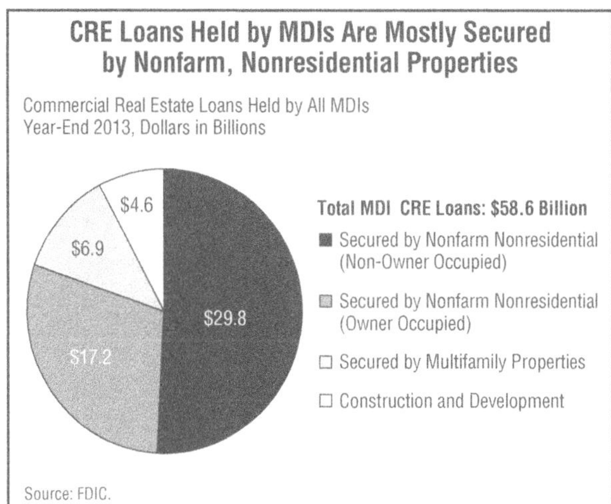


Chart 1.7

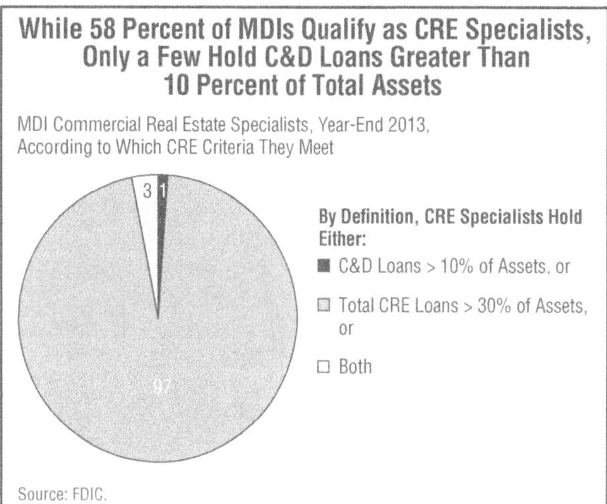


caution. As documented in the *FDIC Community Banking Study*, this type of lending has increased throughout the industry over the past several decades.[11] In addition, in terms of credit losses, these owner-occupied CRE loans performed somewhat better, on average, than unsecured C&I loans in the recent crisis.

The *FDIC Community Banking Study* also indicated that construction and development loans have generally performed worse than other CRE loan types during real estate downturns, and concentrations in construction and development (C&D) lending were associated with higher rates of failure during these periods of adversity. Although MDIs held $4.6 billion in C&D loans as of year-end 2013, few MDIs have concentrations in this type of lending. Only four of the MDIs that met the CRE lending specialist criteria in 2013 had a 10 percent concentration in C&D loans, comprising 4 percent of all MDIs that met the CRE criteria (see Chart 1.7). This is a much smaller percentage than the 16 percent of community bank CRE lenders that had a C&D concentration at year-end 2013.

### *Section Summary*

Over time, a series of legislative, regulatory, and executive actions have been taken to further the goal of ensuring access to financial services by underserved populations and to encourage investment in and support of low- and moderate-income households and communities. Congress has enacted laws to provide a designation process for minority depository institutions as well as a certification process for community development financial institutions. Institutions that meet these definitions may benefit from programs created to support their provision of financial services to underserved consumers and communities.

Compared with the more than 6,800 insured financial institutions, the number of minority depository institutions and insured institutions that are certified as community development financial institutions is quite small. MDIs serve a number of minority groups, with half of MDIs bearing an Asian American minority status, followed by a large share of MDIs with a Hispanic American minority status. Finally, the balance sheet characteristics of MDIs generally resemble those of community banks. The following section considers the geography of MDIs and CDFI banks.

## Section 2. The Geography of MDIs and FDIC-Insured CDFIs

As the report will demonstrate when discussing social performance of minority depository institutions, MDIs are naturally linked to geographic areas that reflect the communities they seek to serve. The 174 MDI headquarters locations are mostly found in a relatively small number of metropolitan areas. However, these same institutions maintain nearly 1,800 offices that are somewhat more widely distributed. This section describes the geographic characteristics of MDI headquarters and office locations, examines their market share, and briefly describes the geographic characteristics of FDIC-insured CDFI institutions.

Map 2.1 highlights a number of regional concentrations of MDI headquarters locations according to their

[11] For an extended discussion of the comparative risks of various types of CRE lending, see Chapter 5 of the *FDIC Community Banking Study*, 2012, http://www.fdic.gov/regulations/resources/cbi/report/CBSI-5.pdf.

Map 2.1

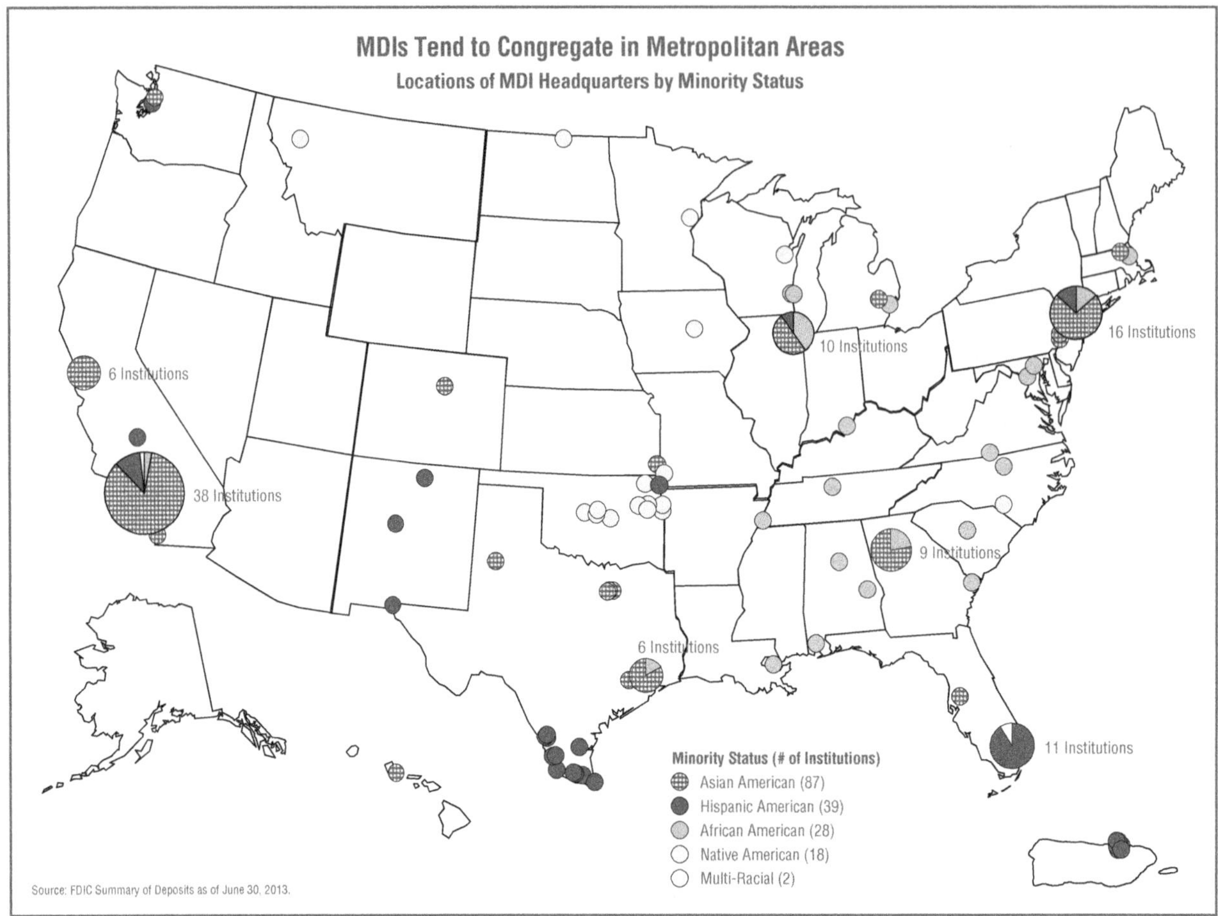


minority status. By way of explanation, the headquarters of MDIs in large metropolitan areas are depicted as pie charts, with the size of the pie increasing with the number of MDIs headquartered in each city and the slices of the pie indicating the breakdown of those institutions by minority status. In the case of metropolitan and nonmetropolitan areas with few MDIs, each headquarters location is shown as a smaller circle. This depiction of MDI headquarters shows a cluster of Hispanic American MDIs in Texas, Florida, and Puerto Rico. African American MDIs tend to be concentrated in the eastern half of the United States, while Native American MDIs are concentrated in Oklahoma and the northern plains.

Overall, more than half of all MDIs reporting at year-end 2013 were headquartered in the four most populous U.S. states: California, Texas, New York, and Florida. California has by far the largest number of MDIs, with the 46 MDIs headquartered there representing more than one-quarter of all MDI charters (see Table 2.1). California is also home to the largest number of MDI offices with 393, or more than one-fifth of all U.S. MDI offices. Texas has the second-largest number of MDI charters with 22 MDI institutions operating 306 banking offices. Puerto Rico only has five MDIs, but it is also home to a total of 389 MDI banking offices, representing 22 percent of all U.S. MDI offices at year-end 2013.

Map 2.1 also shows that MDI headquarters tend to be concentrated in metropolitan areas. In all, some 87 percent of MDI headquarters offices are located in one of the nation's 388 metropolitan areas.[12] In fact, 60 percent

[12] The Office of Management and Budget delineates metropolitan, micropolitan, and combined statistical areas. A revised delineation was issued on February 28, 2013, http://www.whitehouse.gov/sites/default/files/omb/bulletins/2013/b13-01.pdf. Metropolitan Statistical Areas have at least one urbanized area of 50,000 or more population, plus adjacent territory that has a high degree of social and economic integration with the core as measured by commuting ties. Micropolitan Statistical Areas have at least one urban cluster of at least 10,000 but less than 50,000 population, plus adjacent territory that has a high degree of social and economic integration with the core as measured by commuting ties.

Table 2.1

| Top Ten MDI Headquarters Locations by State | | | | |
|---|---|---|---|---|
| **State** | **Number of Charters** | **Percent of Charters** | **Number of Offices** | **Percent of Offices** |
| California | 46 | 26% | 393 | 22% |
| Texas | 22 | 13% | 306 | 17% |
| New York | 13 | 7% | 117 | 7% |
| Florida | 12 | 7% | 115 | 6% |
| Oklahoma | 11 | 6% | 86 | 5% |
| Georgia | 10 | 6% | 41 | 2% |
| Illinois | 10 | 6% | 70 | 4% |
| Puerto Rico | 5 | 3% | 389 | 22% |
| Hawaii | 4 | 2% | 32 | 2% |
| *New Jersey | 3 | 2% | 30 | 2% |
| *Guam | 3 | 2% | 20 | 1% |
| *Alabama | 3 | 2% | 10 | 1% |
| *Pennsylvania | 3 | 2% | 7 | 0% |
| *Wisconsin | 3 | 2% | 5 | 0% |
| Other States | 26 | 15% | 172 | 10% |
| **Total** | **174** | **100%** | **1,793** | **100%** |

Source: FDIC.
Note: Headquarters are as of December 31, 2013. Offices are as of June 30, 2013, as reported in the 2013 Summary of Deposits.
Offices include those physically located in each state, as opposed to the number of MDI offices operated by the MDIs headquartered in each state.
*Shaded states tied for the tenth-largest number of charters located in the state.

Table 2.2

| Top Ten MDI Headquarters Locations by Metro Area | | | | |
|---|---|---|---|---|
| **Metro Area** | **Number of Charters** | **Percent of Charters** | **Number of Offices** | **Percent of Offices** |
| Los Angeles-Long Beach-Anaheim, CA | 38 | 22% | 280 | 16% |
| New York-Newark-Jersey City, NY-NJ-PA | 16 | 9% | 147 | 8% |
| Miami-Fort Lauderdale-West Palm Beach, FL | 11 | 6% | 103 | 6% |
| Chicago-Naperville-Elgin, IL-IN-WI | 10 | 6% | 70 | 4% |
| Atlanta-Sandy Springs-Roswell, GA | 9 | 5% | 35 | 2% |
| Houston-The Woodlands-Sugar Land, TX | 6 | 3% | 62 | 3% |
| San Francisco-Oakland-Hayward, CA | 6 | 3% | 56 | 3% |
| San Juan-Carolina-Caguas, PR | 5 | 3% | 268 | 15% |
| Urban Honolulu, HI | 4 | 2% | 24 | 1% |
| *McAllen-Edinburg-Mission, TX | 3 | 2% | 51 | 3% |
| *Dallas-Fort Worth-Arlington, TX | 3 | 2% | 30 | 2% |
| *Oklahoma City, OK | 3 | 2% | 30 | 2% |
| *Laredo, TX | 3 | 2% | 25 | 1% |
| *Philadelphia-Camden-Wilmington, PA-NJ-DE-MD | 3 | 2% | 7 | 0% |
| Other Metros (26) | 31 | 18% | 430 | 24% |
| Nonmetro Areas (17) | 23 | 13% | 175 | 10% |
| **Total** | **174** | **100%** | **1,793** | **100%** |

Source: FDIC.
Note: Headquarters are as of December 31, 2013. Offices are as of June 30, 2013, as reported in the 2013 Summary of Deposits.
*Shaded cities tied for the tenth-largest number of charters located in a metropolitan area.

of all MDI headquarters are located in just 9 cities, and another 46 MDIs are headquartered in 31 other metropolitan areas (see Table 2.2). Among the largest cities, 38 MDIs are headquartered in greater Los Angeles, 16 are headquartered in New York, 11 are headquartered in Miami, and 10 are headquartered in Chicago. The remaining 13 percent of MDI headquarters offices, shown as medium-sized dots on the map, are located in 17 nonmetropolitan areas. Nearly half (48 percent) of these nonmetro institutions are Native American MDIs.

Map 2.2

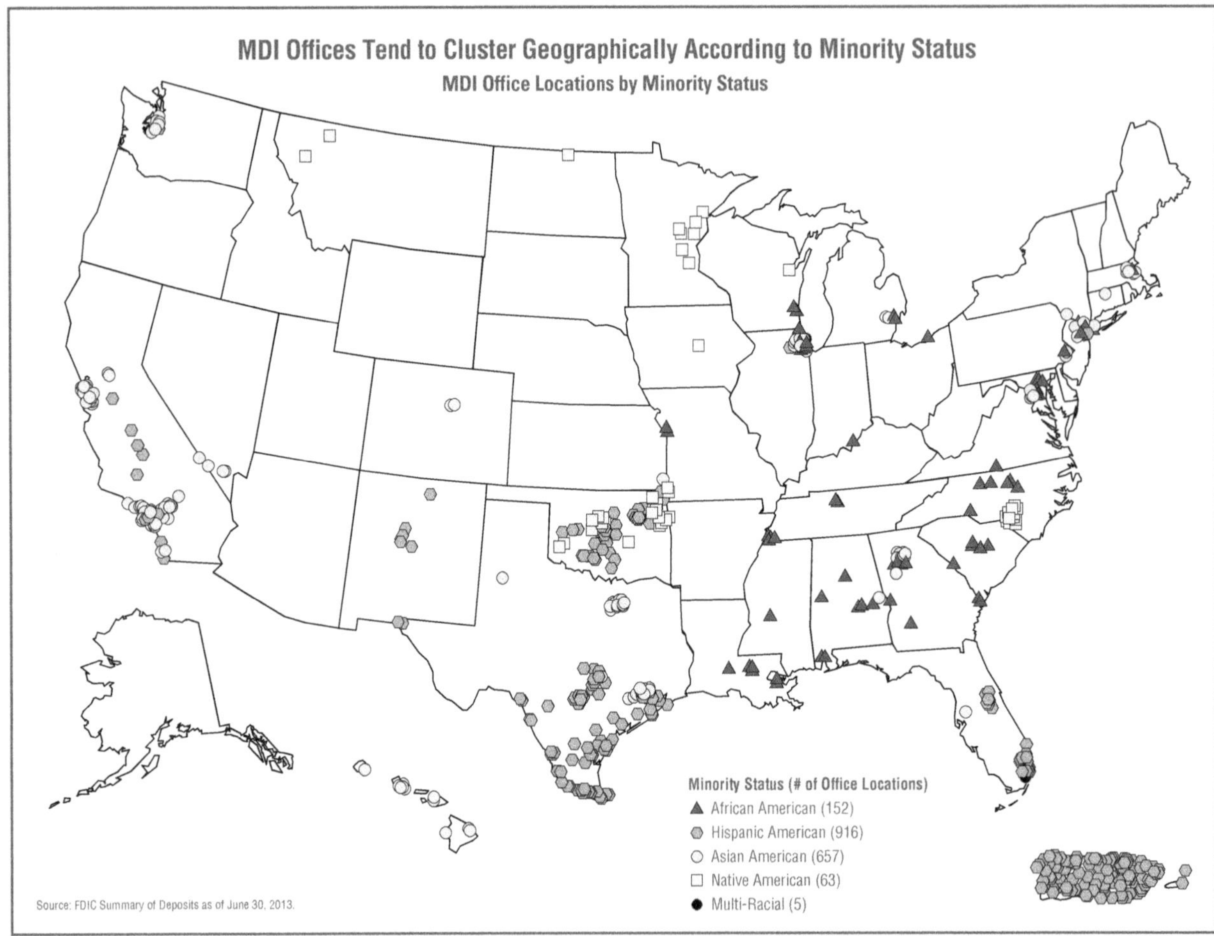


MDI branch offices are similarly distributed across metro and nonmetro areas, with similar geographic concentrations based on minority status (see Map 2.2). Among the 1,793 offices maintained by MDIs as of June 30, 2013, 58 percent were located among the top 9 metro areas shown in Table 2.2, an additional 24 percent were located in 26 other metro areas, and 175 branch offices, or 10 percent, were located in 17 nonmetro areas.

The fact that MDI headquarters and office locations are distributed in a similar fashion across the country is attributable in part to the relatively small geographic footprint of most MDIs. Similar to community banks, MDIs establish branch offices in areas they are familiar with near their headquarters location. Three-fourths of MDIs have offices located in three or fewer counties, compared with 83 percent of community bank offices (see Chart 2.1).

The close proximity of MDI branch offices may also be related to the relatively small number of offices operated by these institutions. With the exception of Hispanic American MDIs, most MDIs have relatively few offices. On average, MDIs serving Asian American, African American, Native American, and multi-racial communities operated fewer than eight offices each (see Chart 2.2). In stark contrast, MDIs that focus on the Hispanic American community tend to operate somewhat larger branch networks. Hispanic American MDIs operated 896 offices in Florida, Oklahoma, Puerto Rico, and Texas, for an average of 24 offices per institution. However, this average is heavily influenced by the 389 MDI banking offices in Puerto Rico. Even when excluding the Puerto Rico MDI offices, Hispanic American MDIs still operate an average of 15 offices per institution, more than twice as many as any other group.

## Market Share

Because so many of their headquarters and branch offices are located in metropolitan areas, MDIs tend to hold a relatively low share of their local banking

Chart 2.1

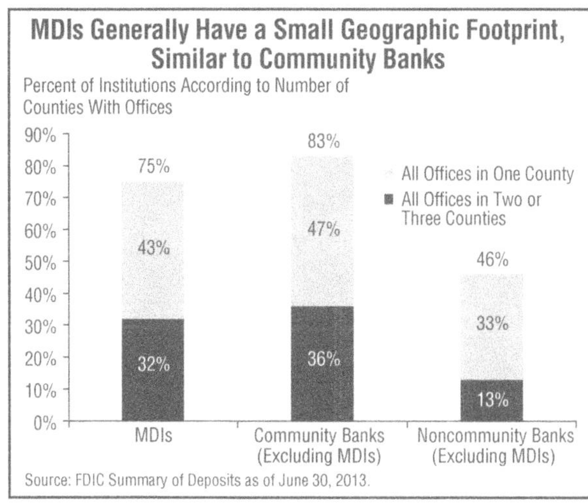


Chart 2.2

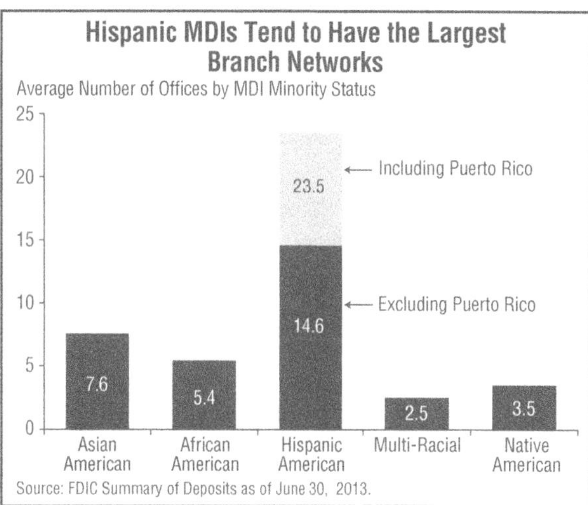


Table 2.3

**Top Ten Large Metro Counties by MDI Deposit Market Share**

| County | Metro | State | MDI Deposits ($000) | MDI Market Share (Percent) |
|---|---|---|---|---|
| Logan | Oklahoma City | OK | $157,368 | 48.3% |
| Webb | Laredo | TX | 2,564,258 | 46.3% |
| Hidalgo | McAllen | TX | 2,590,891 | 26.7% |
| Cameron | Brownsville | TX | 1,024,956 | 24.9% |
| Valencia | Albuquerque | NM | 99,696 | 18.6% |
| Los Angeles | Los Angeles | CA | 30,890,448 | 10.2% |
| Miami-Dade | Miami | FL | 8,328,806 | 8.8% |
| Canadian | Oklahoma City | OK | 118,444 | 7.5% |
| Hoke | Fayetteville | NC | 7,771 | 7.0% |
| DeKalb | Atlanta | GA | 555,792 | 6.8% |
| **Total Metro** | | | **131,792,042** | **1.5%** |

Source: FDIC calculations based on data from the Summary of Deposits and the 2010 Census.

Note: Includes counties of the 50 states and DC with more than 40,000 people in metropolitan areas with total population greater than 250,000. Total Metro includes all counties in metropolitan areas.

market deposits. One way to measure market share is by use of the reported deposits held by individual banking offices as found in the FDIC Summary of Deposits (SOD).[13] MDIs held just 1.5 percent of the metro office deposits of all FDIC-insured institutions in 2013. However, there were four U.S. metropolitan counties that were part of metro areas with populations greater than 250,000 where MDIs held a deposit-market share of at least 25 percent (see Table 2.3).[14] MDIs hold a sizable market share even in some of the largest U.S. metropolitan counties. For instance, they hold more than 10 percent of metro-area deposits in Los Angeles County and nearly 9 percent of metro-area deposits in Miami-Dade County, with combined populations of more than 12 million and MDI deposits of more than $39 billion.

With so many MDIs located in metropolitan areas, micropolitan and rural counties are home to relatively

[13] Data on total banking offices are collected through the Summary of Deposits (SOD), which provides a detailed record of each individual banking office, its location, and total deposits, starting in 1987. The SOD covers all FDIC-insured institutions including insured U.S. branches of foreign banks. Banking offices are defined to include all offices and facilities that actually hold deposits, and do not include loan production offices, computer centers, and other nondeposit installations, such as automated teller machines (ATMs).

[14] These market shares exclude counties in U.S. territories, such as Puerto Rico, where MDIs control more than 90 percent of local deposits in 56 counties.

Table 2.4

| Top Ten Nonmetro Counties by MDI Deposit Market Share | | | | |
|---|---|---|---|---|
| **County** | **Area** | **State** | **MDI Deposits ($000)** | **MDI Market Share (Percent)** |
| Zapata | Micropolitan | TX | $292,612 | 100.0% |
| Starr | Micropolitan | TX | 344,353 | 72.7% |
| Maverick | Micropolitan | TX | 450,900 | 71.7% |
| Adair | Rural | OK | 114,730 | 65.0% |
| Taos | Micropolitan | NM | 162,091 | 38.7% |
| Calhoun | Micropolitan | TX | 147,508 | 33.5% |
| Macon | Rural | AL | 25,788 | 27.8% |
| Jim Hogg | Rural | TX | 41,269 | 25.9% |
| Cherokee | Micropolitan | OK | 98,500 | 25.8% |
| Robeson | Micropolitan | NC | 253,394 | 25.2% |
| **Total Nonmetro** | | | **6,740,152** | **0.9%** |

Source: FDIC calculations based on data from the Summary of Deposits and the 2010 Census.
Note: The list of top ten nonmetro counties excludes counties in U.S. territories. The total MDI market share for nonmetro counties includes counties in U.S. territories.

Table 2.5

| Top Ten Headquarters Locations by State | | | | | | | | |
|---|---|---|---|---|---|---|---|---|
| **MDI Excluding CDFI MDIs** | | | **MDIs That Are Also CDFIs** | | | **Insured CDFIs That Are Not MDIs** | | |
| **State** | **Number of Charters** | **Percent of Charters** | **State** | **Number of Charters** | **Percent of Charters** | **State** | **Number of Charters** | **Percent of Charters** |
| CA | 39 | 29 | CA | 7 | 17 | MS | 12 | 32 |
| TX | 22 | 17 | IL | 7 | 17 | CA | 4 | 11 |
| FL | 12 | 9 | OK | 3 | 7 | IL | 4 | 11 |
| NY | 11 | 8 | GA | 3 | 7 | GA | 2 | 5 |
| OK | 8 | 6 | NY | 2 | 5 | AL | 2 | 5 |
| GA | 7 | 5 | AL | 2 | 5 | OK | 1 | 3 |
| PR | 5 | 4 | PA | 2 | 5 | NY | 1 | 3 |
| HI | 4 | 3 | TN | 2 | 5 | WI | 1 | 3 |
| GU | 3 | 2 | NJ | 1 | 2 | DC | 1 | 3 |
| IL | 3 | 2 | WI | 1 | 2 | KY | 1 | 3 |
| 15 Other States | 19 | 14 | 11 Other States | 11 | 27 | 8 Other States | 8 | 22 |
| **Total** | **133** | **100** | **Total** | **41** | **100** | **Total** | **37** | **100** |

Source: FDIC.
Note: Charters are as of December 31, 2013.

few MDIs, and they hold less than 1 percent of local deposits in these markets. However, there are selected nonmetro areas in which MDIs hold a much larger deposit market share. Excluding U.S. territories, MDIs held more than a 9 percent deposit market share in 27 micropolitan and rural counties in 2013. Many of these counties, such as those in Oklahoma, New Mexico, and Montana, are served by Native American institutions. The top ten nonmetro counties by MDI deposit market share are shown in Table 2.4.

### FDIC-Insured CDFI Locations Differ From Non-CDFI MDI Markets

In 2013, there were 37 FDIC-insured institutions certified as CDFIs that were not also designated as minority depository institutions. These non-MDI CDFI banks have a geographic footprint that differs from most MDIs. Whereas most MDIs are highly concentrated in the four most populous states, the 37 FDIC-insured CDFIs that are not MDIs are concentrated in Mississippi, Illinois, and California (see Table 2.5). Together,

Table 2.6

| Top Ten Office Locations by State | | | | | | | | |
|---|---|---|---|---|---|---|---|---|
| MDI Excluding CDFI MDIs | | | MDIs That Are Also CDFIs | | | Insured CDFIs That Are Not MDIs | | |
| State | Number of Offices | Percent of Offices | State | Number of Offices | Percent of Offices | State | Number of Offices | Percent of Offices |
| PR | 389 | 24 | IL | 41 | 20 | MS | 185 | 56 |
| CA | 364 | 23 | CA | 29 | 14 | AL | 27 | 8 |
| TX | 306 | 19 | NY | 25 | 12 | AR | 23 | 7 |
| FL | 114 | 7 | GA | 18 | 9 | IL | 12 | 4 |
| NY | 92 | 6 | LA | 12 | 6 | LA | 12 | 4 |
| OK | 81 | 5 | MD | 9 | 4 | SC | 12 | 4 |
| HI | 32 | 2 | AL | 8 | 4 | GA | 10 | 3 |
| IL | 29 | 2 | NC | 8 | 4 | CA | 9 | 3 |
| NJ | 24 | 2 | DC | 6 | 3 | MN | 8 | 2 |
| GA | 23 | 1 | NJ | 6 | 3 | OR | 6 | 2 |
| 25 Other States | 136 | 9 | 16 Other States | 41 | 20 | 11 Other States | 27 | 8 |
| **Total** | **1,590** | **100** | **Total** | **203** | **100** | **Total** | **331** | **100** |
| Average Number of Offices Per Charter: | | 12.0 | Average Number of Offices Per Charter: | | 5.0 | Average Number of Offices Per Charter: | | 8.9 |
| | Excl. PR | 9.4 | | | | | | |

Source: FDIC.
Note: Charters are as of December 31, 2013.

Table 2.7

| Location of Charter by Metro and Nonmetro Area | | | | | | |
|---|---|---|---|---|---|---|
| | MDI Excluding CDFI MDIs | | MDIs That Are Also CDFIs | | Insured CDFIs That Are Not MDIs | |
| Area | Number of Charters | Percent of Charters | Number of Charters | Percent of Charters | Number of Charters | Percent of Charters |
| Metro | 115 | 86.5 | 36 | 87.8 | 19 | 51.4 |
| Nonmetro | 18 | 13.5 | 5 | 12.2 | 18 | 48.6 |
| **Total** | **133** | **100** | **41** | **100** | **37** | **100** |

Source: FDIC.
Note: Charters are as of December 31, 2013.

these states represent more than half (54 percent) of all non-MDI FDIC-insured CDFI charters.

Not only are non-MDI FDIC-insured CDFIs concentrated in a few states, but more than half of their banking offices are located in Mississippi. This is in part due to the larger size and branching network of Mississippi banks that are certified as CDFIs, as well as the higher percentage of low-income households in Mississippi. (Among all states, Mississippi has the highest percentage population living below the poverty level.) The 12 FDIC-insured CDFIs headquartered in Mississippi have on average 15 offices each (see Table 2.6).

Non-MDI CDFI banks also differ from MDIs in terms of the share located in nonmetropolitan areas. While almost 90 percent of MDIs are headquartered in metro areas, only about half (51.4 percent) of non-MDI FDIC-insured CDFIs are headquartered in metro areas (see Table 2.7).

*Section Summary*

Minority depository institutions are naturally linked to geographic areas that reflect the communities they seek to serve. As a result, most MDIs are headquartered in a handful of the most populous states. In addition, a large majority of the headquarters and branch offices of these institutions are located in large metropolitan areas. Due to the concentration of MDI headquarters and branch offices in large metro areas, MDIs generally hold a relatively small share of their local market. Nonetheless, there are a few large counties, including Los Angeles and Miami-Dade, where MDIs hold a rather significant share of total bank deposits. Minority depository institutions also hold a sizable share of deposits in some micropolitan and rural counties, although their overall presence in nonmetro areas is small. The concentration of MDI offices in a limited number of metropolitan areas is to some extent attributable to the relatively small geographic footprint of MDIs, with most MDI offices being located in an area of three counties or less. With the exception of Hispanic American MDIs, most MDIs operate a relatively small number of banking offices.

Unlike MDIs, insured institutions that are certified as CDFIs, but are not also MDIs, tend to be concentrated in Mississippi, Illinois, and California, with more than half of their banking offices located in Mississippi. Finally, unlike MDIs, only about half of these FDIC-insured CDFIs are located in metropolitan areas.

## Section 3. Structural Change Among Minority Depository Institutions

The financial services industry has experienced significant change over the past three decades as a result of failures, mergers between banking organizations, the consolidation of charters within existing organizations, and newly chartered institutions. During the 13-year study period covered by the report, the MDI sector has also experienced a great deal of structural change. Not only has it experienced even greater structural change than community banks as a whole during this period, but the sources of this change have been somewhat unique to the MDI sector. This section further details the nature of structural change in the MDI sector between 2001 and 2013.

### Number of Charters

During the study period, MDIs increased in absolute number, from 164 charters in 2001 to 174 in 2013. As previously noted, MDI assets have more than doubled over this period, from $83 billion to $181 billion. However, as reflected in Chart 3.1, the size of the MDI sector peaked near the beginning of the recent financial crisis, and has trended downward since that time in both absolute and relative terms.

The decline in the size of the MDI sector is related to a number of factors, the most important of which has been bank failures. Over the entire study period, MDIs were about three times as likely to fail as all other banks. Between year-end 2001 and 2013, 33 MDIs failed (see Chart 3.2, lower right). The number of MDI charters has also declined as a result of voluntary mergers. During the study period, 29 MDIs were acquired by non-MDI financial institutions, and an additional 28 MDIs were acquired by other MDIs (lower left). There has also been a sharp slowdown in the chartering of new MDIs, with only 6 being created since 2007, whereas 33 new MDIs were chartered between 2005 and 2007 (upper left).

Over the past 13 years, a large number of preexisting institutions were designated as MDIs, while fewer institutions lost MDI status (Chart 3.2, upper right). This

Chart 3.1

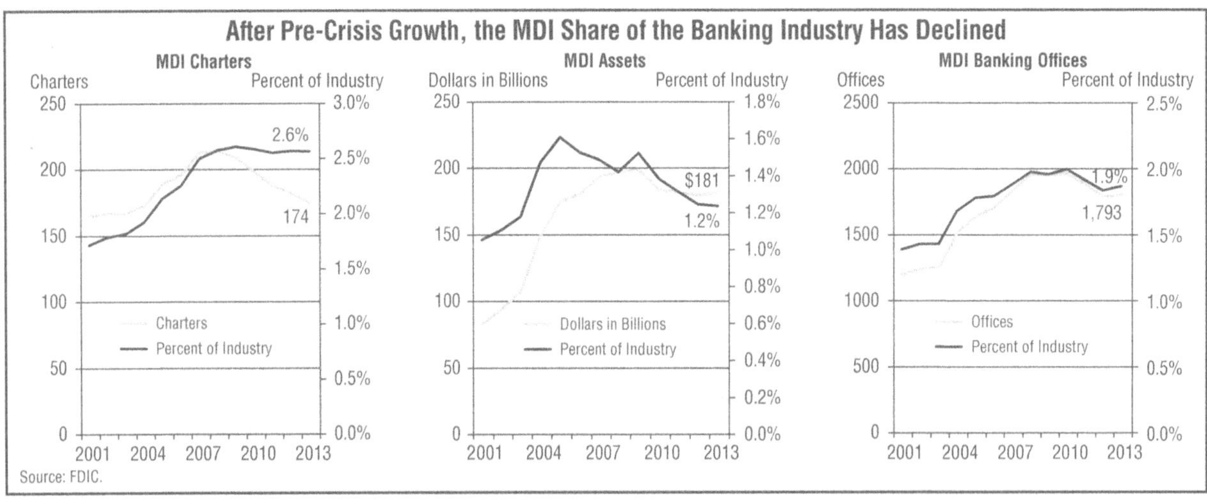

Chart 3.2

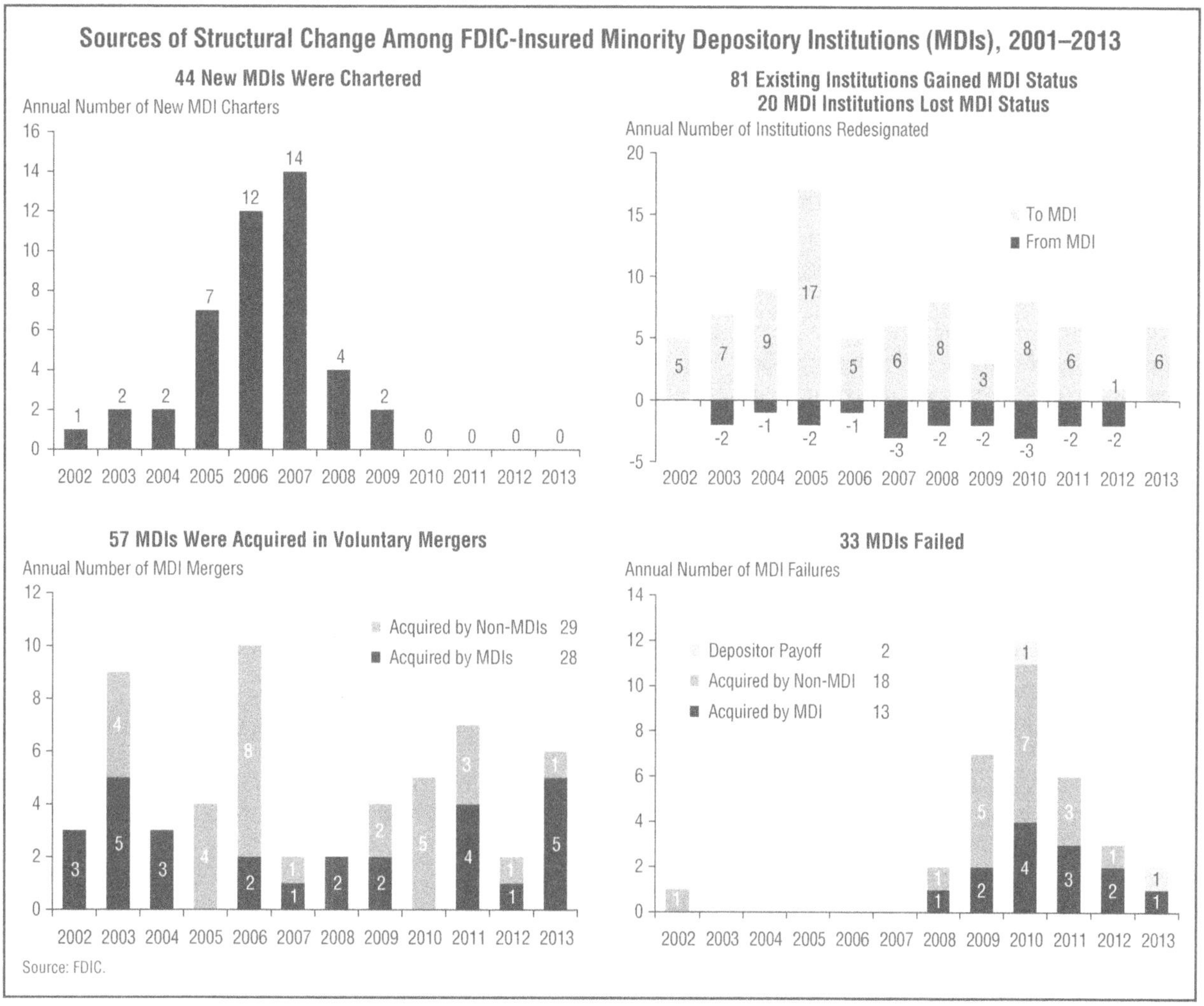

**Sources of Structural Change Among FDIC-Insured Minority Depository Institutions (MDIs), 2001–2013**

**44 New MDIs Were Chartered**

Annual Number of New MDI Charters

| | 2002 | 2003 | 2004 | 2005 | 2006 | 2007 | 2008 | 2009 | 2010 | 2011 | 2012 | 2013 |
|---|---|---|---|---|---|---|---|---|---|---|---|---|
| New MDI Charters | 1 | 2 | 2 | 7 | 12 | 14 | 4 | 2 | 0 | 0 | 0 | 0 |

**81 Existing Institutions Gained MDI Status**
**20 MDI Institutions Lost MDI Status**

Annual Number of Institutions Redesignated

| | 2002 | 2003 | 2004 | 2005 | 2006 | 2007 | 2008 | 2009 | 2010 | 2011 | 2012 | 2013 |
|---|---|---|---|---|---|---|---|---|---|---|---|---|
| To MDI | 5 | 7 | 9 | 17 | 5 | 6 | 8 | 3 | 8 | 6 | 1 | 6 |
| From MDI | | -2 | -1 | -2 | -1 | -3 | -2 | -2 | -3 | -2 | -2 | |

**57 MDIs Were Acquired in Voluntary Mergers**

Annual Number of MDI Mergers

Acquired by Non-MDIs 29
Acquired by MDIs 28

| | 2002 | 2003 | 2004 | 2005 | 2006 | 2007 | 2008 | 2009 | 2010 | 2011 | 2012 | 2013 |
|---|---|---|---|---|---|---|---|---|---|---|---|---|
| Acquired by Non-MDIs | | 4 | | 4 | 8 | 1 | | 2 | 5 | 3 | 1 | 1 |
| Acquired by MDIs | 3 | 5 | 3 | | 2 | 1 | 2 | 2 | | 4 | 1 | 5 |

**33 MDIs Failed**

Annual Number of MDI Failures

Depositor Payoff 2
Acquired by Non-MDI 18
Acquired by MDI 13

| | 2002 | 2003 | 2004 | 2005 | 2006 | 2007 | 2008 | 2009 | 2010 | 2011 | 2012 | 2013 |
|---|---|---|---|---|---|---|---|---|---|---|---|---|
| Depositor Payoff | 1 | | | | | | | | 1 | | | |
| Acquired by Non-MDI | | | | | | | 1 | 5 | 7 | 3 | 1 | 1 |
| Acquired by MDI | | | | | | | 1 | 2 | 4 | 3 | 2 | 1 |

Source: FDIC.

was the most important source of growth for the MDI sector over much of the study period.

Chart 3.3 depicts the net effect of new charters, mergers, failures, and redesignations over the study period. A total of 81 institutions were redesignated as MDIs during the study period, compared with 20 institutions that lost MDI status, making redesignation the most important factor behind the net increase in the number of MDIs over the study period.

Chart 3.3

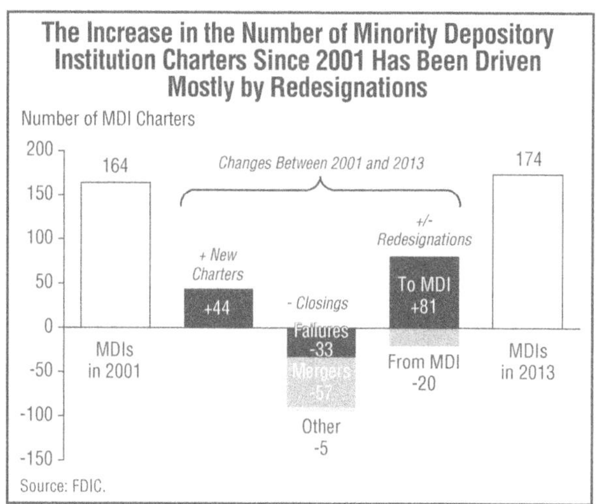


## Impact of Structural Change on the Assets Controlled by MDIs

As minority depository institutions have failed or merged, concerns have been expressed that these institutions are being acquired by entities that may not be focused on addressing the financial needs of minority communities. Indeed, one of the stated goals of Section 308 of the Financial Institutions Reform, Recovery, and Enforcement Act is to "preserve the minority character in cases of merger or acquisition." But despite acquisition of 88 MDIs during the study period, most of the assets of these institutions have been acquired by other MDIs (see Chart 3.4). Of the 57 MDIs acquired through voluntary mergers during the study period, slightly less than half (28 institutions) were acquired by other MDIs. In addition, of the 33 MDIs that failed during the study period, 13 (39 percent) were acquired by other MDIs. Although these percentages might appear low at first glance, it is important to point out that a much larger share of the total assets of closed MDIs remained under the control of other MDIs after acquisition. In all, nearly two-thirds of the assets of the merged institutions and 87 percent of the assets of the failed institutions wound up staying with MDI acquirers.

While every segment of the banking industry has undergone structural change in recent years, the MDI population has been relatively volatile compared with other types of institutions. For example, MDIs were about half as likely as community banks as a whole to operate continuously (that is, in the absence of structural change or group redesignation) throughout the study period (see Chart 3.5). Only 30 percent of MDIs operated continuously throughout the study period, compared with 57 percent of community banks. This volatility in the MDI population tends to complicate time series analysis, as changes in the population sometimes matter as much or more than changes in performance.

## Changes in Minority Status Designation

As the MDI sector has changed over time, so has its composition in terms of minority status. The most prominent change to this composition has been the increase in the share of MDIs that have an Asian American minority status. Since 2001, the number of MDIs with this minority status increased by about a third. By 2013, Asian American institutions represented half of all MDIs (see Chart 3.6). The number of Hispanic American MDIs grew from 23 institutions in 2001 to 34 in 2013, representing 19.5 percent of MDI charters. Meanwhile, the number of African American MDIs declined by more than one-third during this period and they represented fewer than one-fifth of all MDIs at year-end 2013, compared with nearly a third of all MDIs in 2001.

Chart 3.4

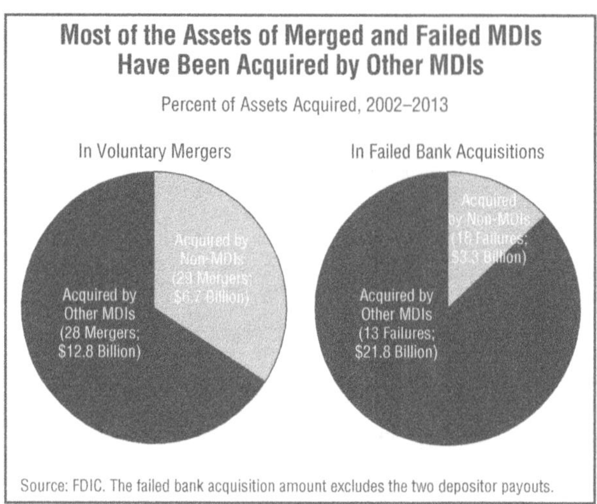


Chart 3.5

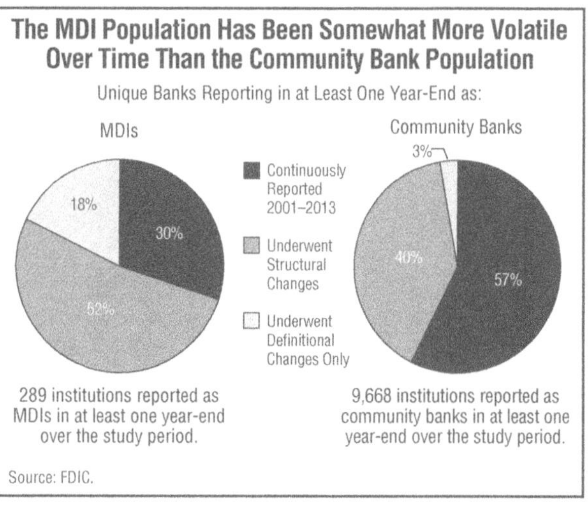


Chart 3.6

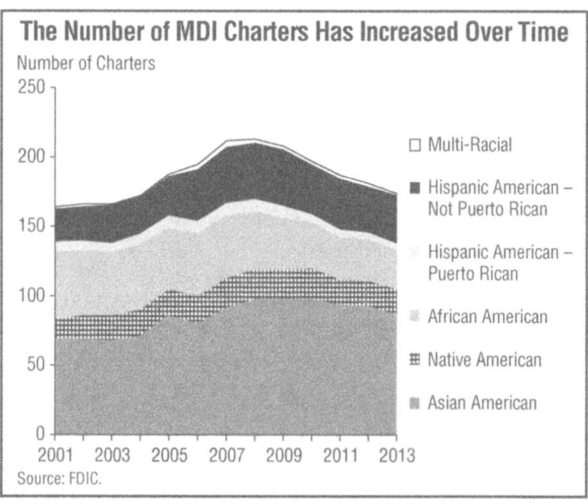

As the composition of MDI minority status groups changed over the period, the share of MDI assets also shifted. In 2001, Asian American institutions held 23 percent of MDI assets. By year-end 2013, their share of MDI assets had nearly doubled to 43 percent. The assets of Hispanic American MDIs also grew rapidly, rising more than two-thirds during the study period and leaving them with 52 percent of total MDI assets in 2013. Hispanic American MDIs in Puerto Rico made up over one-third of total MDI assets in 2013. Finally, African American, Native American, and Multi-Racial MDIs held 4 percent or less of MDI assets at year-end 2013.

### *Section Summary*

Like other groups of depository institutions, the MDI banking segment experienced significant structural change during the 2001–2013 period of this study. The number of MDI charters has fluctuated as new MDIs were chartered, existing institutions were designated as MDIs, existing MDIs were acquired by other institutions, and some MDIs failed. In fact, compared with the industry overall, and especially community banks, the MDI population has experienced significant volatility, with relatively few MDIs operating continuously throughout the study period. The composition of the MDI segment has also changed over time, as the share of MDIs with an Asian American or Hispanic American minority status has increased and the share of African American MDIs has declined.

## Section 4. Financial Performance of Minority Depository Institutions

As described in earlier sections, the MDI segment is relatively small, with only 174 out of 6,812 FDIC-insured institutions being designated as MDIs at year-end 2013. In addition, this industry segment has changed significantly during the study period and has demonstrated greater volatility than other industry segments. These factors make long-term group comparisons of MDI performance difficult. Nonetheless, it is instructive to compare the relative performance of MDIs with other groups of institutions, both in terms of standard measures of financial performance (this section) and in terms of social impact (Section 5). This section describes the financial performance of MDIs between year-end 2001 and year-end 2013, compared with two groups: community and noncommunity banks that are not designated as MDIs (so-called non-MDI community banks and non-MDI noncommunity banks). Section 2 has already described how MDIs more closely resemble community banks than noncommunity banks in terms of size and balance sheet characteristics.

Chart 4.1

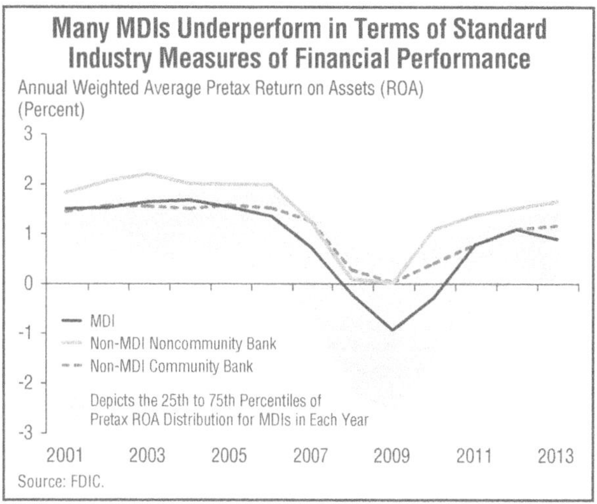


This section finds that while the financial performance of MDIs also more closely resembles that of community banks than noncommunity banks, MDIs tend to underperform both groups in terms of standard measures of financial performance. Several factors that may contribute to this difference in performance are also explored, including the concentration of MDIs in metropolitan areas, many of which experienced extreme financial distress during the recession, as well as the relatively young age of MDIs.

### Profitability

One of the most widely used measures of financial institution performance is pretax return on assets (pretax ROA).[15] Chart 4.1 depicts annual pretax ROA for MDIs and non-MDI community and noncommunity institutions over the 2001–2013 period. The shaded region on the chart also depicts the 25th to 75th percentile of the pretax ROA distribution for MDIs in each year, with the bottom and top 25 percent of MDIs excluded.

Across the entire study period, MDIs reported a weighted average pretax ROA of 0.69 percent, compared with 1.02 percent for community banks and 1.34 percent for noncommunity banks. The average profitability of MDIs and community banks was very similar through roughly the first five to six years of this period, after which MDIs began to underperform both community and noncommunity banks. However, MDI profitability once again converged with that of community banks in

[15] Pretax return on assets equals pretax net income as a percent of average assets and includes extraordinary items and other adjustments, net of taxes.

Chart 4.2

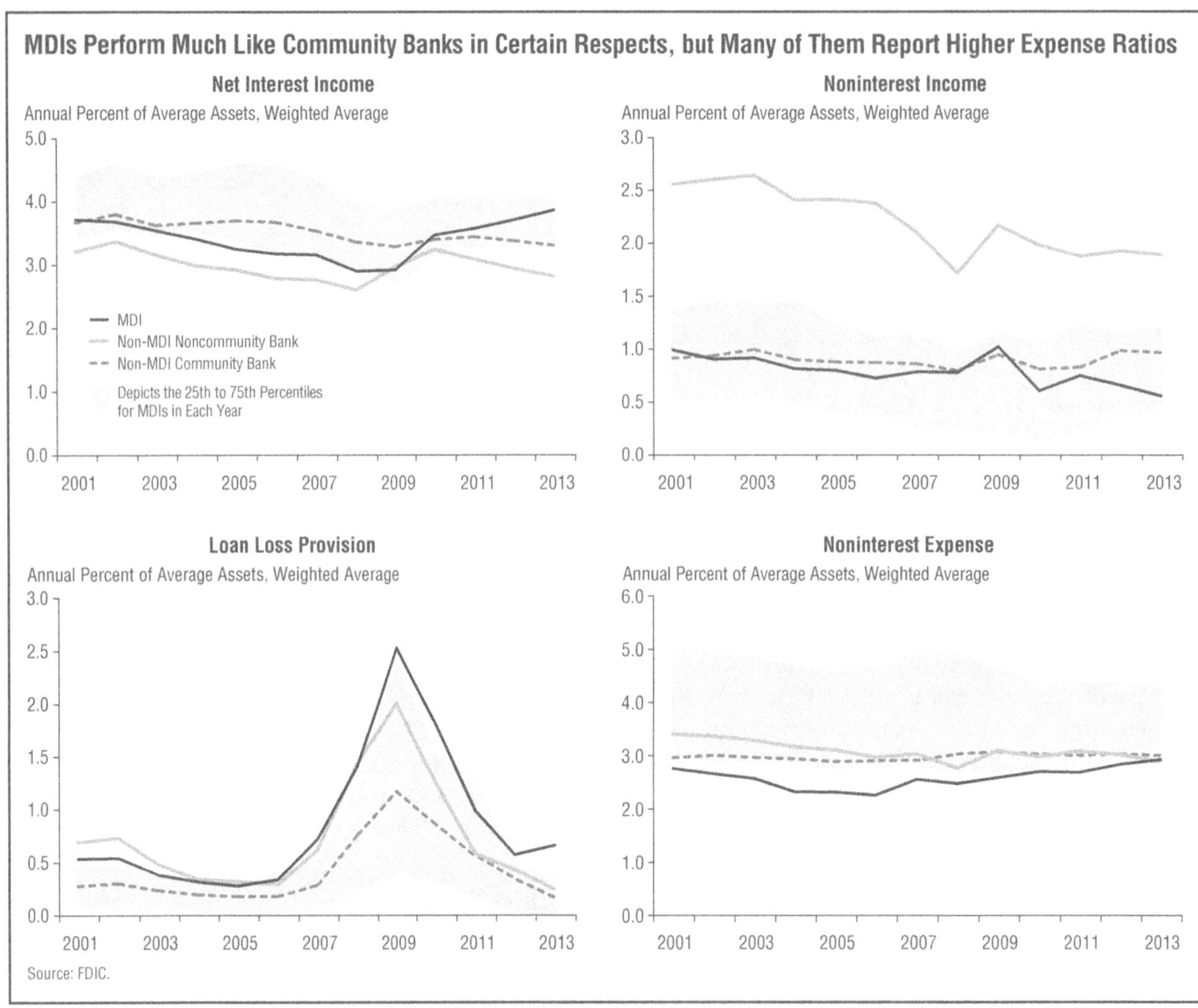


2011 and 2012 as the economy recovered and asset quality stabilized.

Although MDIs were found to perform somewhat like community banks with regard to net interest income and noninterest income (see Chart 4.2, upper charts), MDIs experienced higher expenses related to problem loans, as well as higher overhead expenses. For example, across the study period, MDIs reported loan loss provisions averaging 0.93 percent of assets, more than twice as much as community banks and higher even than noncommunity banks (lower left). Meanwhile, MDIs reported overhead expenses that were lower, on average, than both community and noncommunity banks (lower right). However, the shaded region in the noninterest expense chart shows that almost three-quarters of MDIs reported above average expense ratios in any given year. The very smallest MDIs, in particular, were found to have much-higher-than-average overhead expenses. Across the study period, MDIs under $100 million reported noninterest expenses that were more than twice as high (4.8 percent) as those reported by MDIs over $1 billion (2.3 percent).

The influence of minority status and institution size may also help to explain variation in expense and efficiency ratios across MDI minority status groups. As shown in Chart 4.3, overhead expenses have been substantially higher among African American, Native American and Multi-Racial MDIs than among Asian American and Hispanic American MDIs. Although geography may be one factor that drives these disparities—for example, MDIs in Puerto Rico have much lower expense ratios than those in New York—the most important factor seems to be average size. The African American, Native American, and Multi-Racial MDIs average $100 to $250 million in size in

Chart 4.3

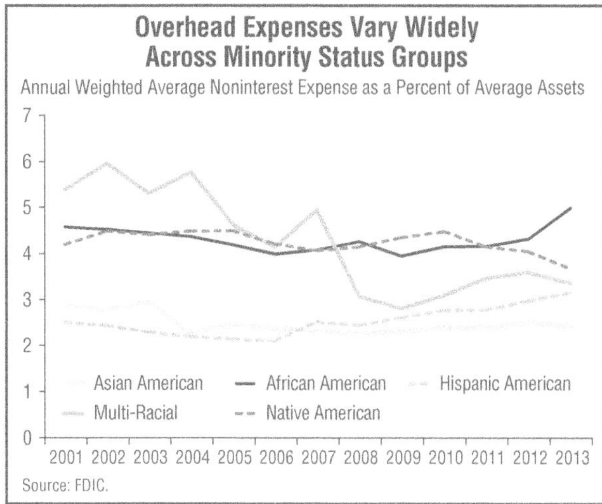


Chart 4.4

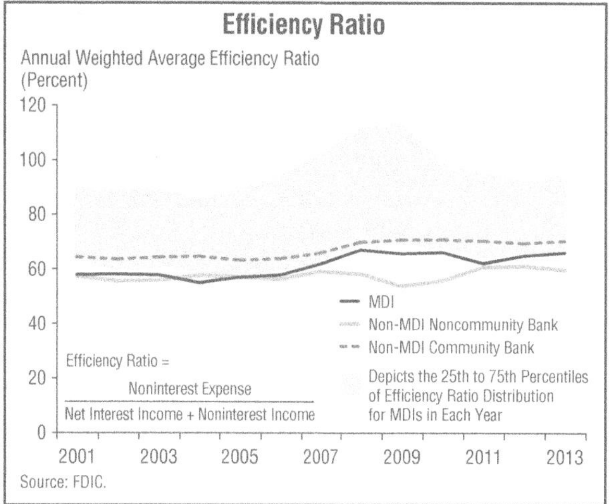


2013—far smaller than the $900 million for Asian American MDIs and $1 billion for Hispanic American MDIs outside Puerto Rico. Puerto Rico MDIs averaged $11.9 billion in assets at year-end 2013.

Efficiency ratios also show differences in the ability of small and large banks to generate revenue in relation to the expenses they incur in doing so. The efficiency ratio is the ratio of noninterest expense to net operating revenue, where a higher efficiency ratio indicates an institution that is less efficient at generating revenue per dollar of noninterest expense.[16] The *FDIC Community Banking Study* identified the emergence of a sizable "efficiency gap" between community and noncommunity banks during the period after 1998 that has narrowed only slightly in the years following the onset of the recent financial crisis. In comparison, the average MDI efficiency ratio has tended to fall between the weighted average for community and noncommunity banks (see Chart 4.4). During the study period, the average efficiency ratio of noncommunity banks equaled 57.1 percent, compared with 61.4 percent for MDIs, and 66.6 percent for community banks. Although the weighted average MDI efficiency ratios fell between these two figures during most years, the shaded region on the chart shows that three-quarters or more of MDIs report efficiency ratios higher than the average MDI in any given year.

The large share of MDIs with relatively high efficiency ratios mostly appears to point to higher-than-average

Chart 4.5

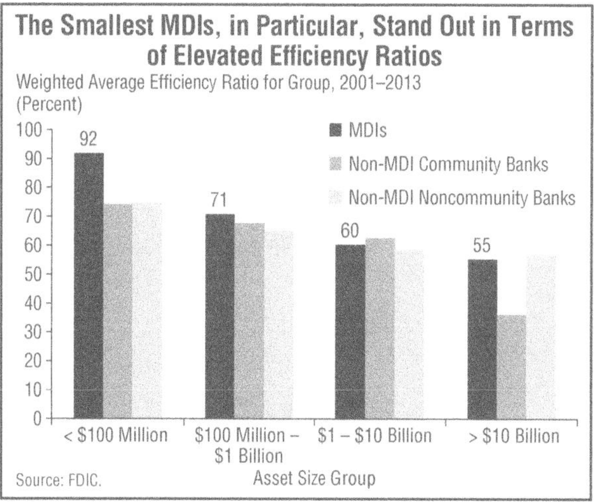


overhead expenses on the part of smaller institutions. Across the study period, MDIs with assets less than $100 million reported an average efficiency ratio (92 percent) that was substantially higher than MDIs with assets over $10 billion (55 percent). While efficiency ratios are generally higher for smaller institutions in every group, the disparity in efficiency ratios by size is even more pronounced in the case of MDIs (see Chart 4.5).

Based on the similarities between MDI and community bank pretax return on assets during most periods, a question arises as to whether the performance differences are statistically significant. The inset box discusses two tests of statistical significance with respect to MDIs and community banks from our observational study completed in 2013.

16 Formally, the efficiency ratio is expressed as:

$$\text{Efficiency Ratio} = \frac{\text{Noninterest Expense}}{\text{Net Interest Income} + \text{Noninterest Income}}$$

## *Are Differences in Financial Performance of MDI and Non-MDI Financial Institutions Statistically Significant?*

In a simple comparison of financial performance, the pretax ROA of MDIs in Chart 4.1 is generally lower than that of non-MDI community banks. Other measures of financial performance depicted in Charts 4.2 through 4.4 also depict systematic differences between the two subject groups. Our analytical work related to the 2013 Interagency MDI/CDFI Bank Conference included analysis of these differences for the period between 2001 and 2012. But are these differences statistically significant?

To answer this question, we conducted an observational study in which financial institutions are treated as subjects and the MDI designation serves as a treatment factor. In this analysis, we employ two tests: a t-test and a Wilcoxon rank-sum test. Both tests have been applied to group comparisons of pretax ROA and other financial performance ratios on a pooled basis over the 2001–2012 period (see Chart below). The t-tests and Wilcoxon rank-sum tests both consistently indicate that differences in financial performance between MDIs and non-MDI community banks are statistically significant. MDIs tend to have measurably lower pretax ROA than do non-MDI community banks, and also have higher noninterest expenses and loan loss provisions. Differences in MDI and non-MDI efficiency ratios were also found to be statistically significant. Overall, the results of our analysis indicate that statistically meaningful differences exist between the financial performance of MDIs and non-MDI community banks.

Additional information related to these tests and the methodology is available in the Appendix.

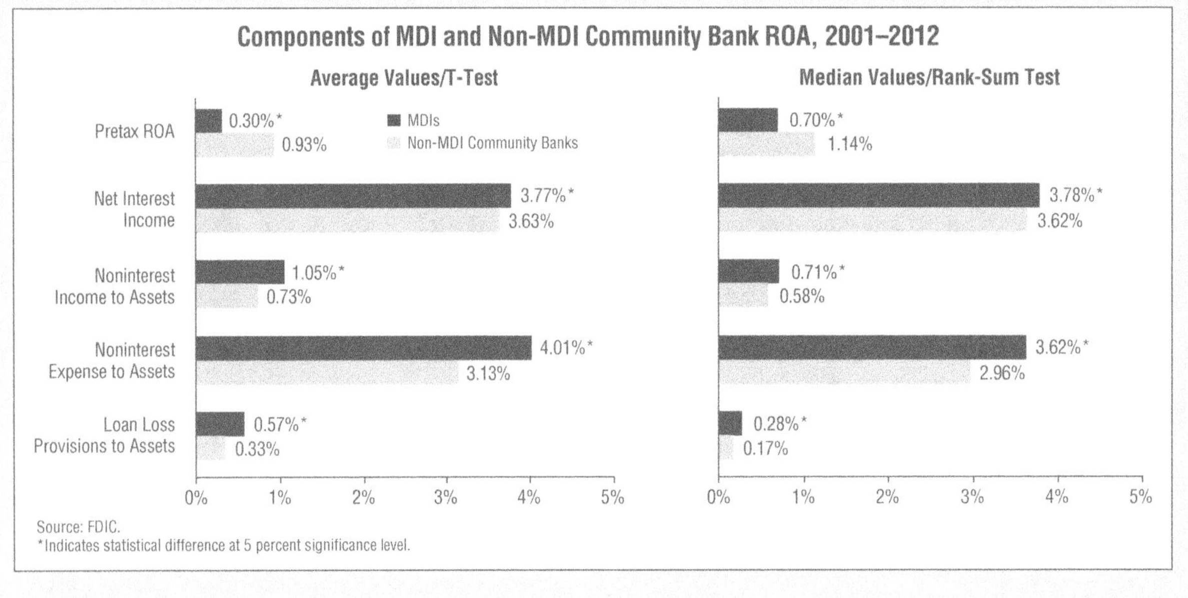


## Factors That Affect Performance

While MDI financial performance resembled that of community banks prior to the recent recession, their performance diverged during the crisis. Table 4.1 shows that the aggregate average pretax return on assets for non-MDI and MDI community banks was similar prior to the crisis, but MDI community banks experienced negative pretax ROA in the period from 2007 to 2009. These results do not necessarily rule out the possibility of other correlating factors. Future research may provide additional insight into these potential correlations, which could include geographic and age characteristics.

Some of the difference in MDI and non-MDI performance may be attributed to the influence of geographic concentrations. As noted earlier, 60 percent of MDI offices were located among the top nine metro areas, with many of these large metro areas experiencing severe distress during the economic crisis. Table 4.1 shows that both MDI and non-MDI community banks headquartered in metro areas had lower pretax ROA during the recession, compared with institutions in nonmetro areas.

Younger institutions also performed worse relative to more seasoned charters. Overall, MDIs have a higher

Table 4.1

| MDI Performance Resembles Similarly Situated Community Banks | | | | | | | |
|---|---|---|---|---|---|---|---|
| Aggregate Average Pretax Return on Assets, Percent | | | | | | | |
| **Overall** | | **2001–2003** | **2004–2006** | **2007–2009** | **2010–2012** | **2013** | **2001–2013** |
| Noncommunity Banks | | | | | | | |
| Non-MDI | | 2.0 | 2.0 | 0.4 | 1.3 | 1.6 | 1.3 |
| MDI | | 1.6 | 1.5 | -0.1 | 0.6 | 0.9 | 0.8 |
| Community Banks | | | | | | | |
| Non-MDI | | 1.5 | 1.5 | 0.5 | 0.7 | 1.1 | 1.0 |
| MDI | | 1.3 | 1.5 | -0.5 | 0.1 | 0.8 | 0.5 |
| **By MSA** | | | | | | | |
| Community Banks | | | | | | | |
| Non-MDI | Metro | 1.5 | 1.5 | 0.3 | 0.6 | 1.1 | 0.9 |
| | Nonmetro | 1.5 | 1.5 | 0.9 | 0.9 | 1.2 | 1.2 |
| MDI | Metro | 1.3 | 1.6 | -0.6 | 0.1 | 0.8 | 0.5 |
| | Nonmetro | 1.3 | 1.4 | 0.6 | 0.8 | 0.8 | 0.9 |
| **By Age** | | | | | | | |
| Community Banks | | | | | | | |
| Non-MDI | Less Than 5 Years | 0.2 | 0.2 | 0.1 | 0.3 | 0.4 | 0.2 |
| | 5 - 10 Years | 1.3 | 1.4 | 0.0 | 0.3 | 1.0 | 0.7 |
| | Over 10 Years | 1.6 | 1.6 | 0.5 | 0.8 | 1.1 | 1.1 |
| MDI | Less Than 5 Years | -0.2 | 0.5 | -1.9 | 0.3 | -1.2 | -0.6 |
| | 5 - 10 Years | 1.2 | 1.4 | -0.6 | 0.0 | 1.5 | 0.3 |
| | Over 10 Years | 1.3 | 1.6 | -0.4 | 0.2 | 0.8 | 0.6 |

Source: FDIC.

proportion of younger institutions than do non-MDIs. The 2012 *FDIC Community Banking Study* demonstrated that newer community banks on average underperformed more mature community banks. In nearly every time period studied, community banks with an age of less than five years performed worse than any other age cohort. This phenomenon is consistent among young MDI community banks as well. Younger MDIs had lower pretax ROA both leading up to as well as during the recession.

*Section Summary*

The wide variation in size among MDI institutions, in addition to significant structural change in this segment, tends to complicate long-term group comparisons of MDI performance with that of other groups of banks. Nonetheless, we find that MDIs generally underperform non-MDI community and noncommunity institutions in terms of standard industry measures of financial performance such as pretax return on assets. MDIs were found to perform much like community banks with regard to net interest income and noninterest income, but experienced higher expenses related to problem loans as well as higher overhead expenses. Smaller MDIs especially were found to have much higher noninterest expenses compared with larger MDIs and community banks. In addition, smaller MDIs also were less efficient compared with both mid-size and larger MDIs, as well as non-MDI community and noncommunity banks. However, to the extent that MDIs have been chartered to serve a variety of stakeholders in addition to equity shareholders, it is important to also consider their relative performance in terms of social impact, which we do in Section 5.

## Section 5. Social Impact of Minority Depository Institutions

MDIs play an important role in providing mortgage credit and other banking services to minority and low- and moderate-income (LMI) communities.[17] As noted in Section 2, MDI headquarters are concentrated in metropolitan areas, while their 1,793 offices are somewhat more widely distributed. There is a natural

[17] Low-income census tracts have median family income of less than 50 percent of the MSA's median family income. Moderate-income census tracts have median family income of between 50 percent and less than 80 percent of the MSA's median family income.

## *Estimating the Service Area of Each Bank*

To examine the impact of MDIs on the communities they serve, it is necessary to first identify the *geographic service area* of each bank. Unfortunately, there are no readily available data indicating each bank's self-identified market area. In addition, the availability of data indicating a bank's Community Reinvestment Act (CRA) assessment area is subject to a *de minimis* test, and is therefore incomplete. Some previous researchers have estimated bank service areas as simply the sum of the census tracts in which each bank operates headquarters and branch offices. A shortcoming of this approach is that a census tract often covers only a small geographic area, and the average size of census tracts tends to decline as population density increases. In addition, looking only at the census tracts in which a bank's offices are located ignores people living in other nearby tracts who may also be served by those offices.

This report employs a novel computation of the service area of each bank that also includes census tracts *adjacent to* and *nearby* those in which the bank's offices are located. The following two-step process is used to identify the geographic service area of each bank:

**Step 1: Determine a "reasonable distance" for customers to travel to do their banking business in a given metropolitan or nonmetropolitan area.** For each geographic area, the reasonable distance is computed such that roughly 90 percent of the area's population has at least one full-service bank branch within that distance. Generally this reasonable distance is substantially longer for nonmetropolitan areas than it is for more densely populated metropolitan areas. Moreover, reasonable distances can differ substantially across various metro and nonmetro areas located around the country. For example, using 2011 data from the FDIC Summary of Deposits, New York City had the shortest reasonable distance of any MSA (0.6 miles), while Flagstaff, Arizona, had the longest reasonable distance (22.5 miles). For nonmetro areas, which are calculated on a statewide basis, reasonable distances based on 2011 data ranged from a low of 1.9 miles in Massachusetts to a high of 66.2 miles in Alaska.

**Step 2: Estimate the service area of each banking office based on this "reasonable distance."** Using the reasonable distance calculation made for each metro or nonmetro area, a circle can be drawn around each banking office located there. Census tracts within or touching that circle are said to be served by that banking office, and the total population served by each banking office is the sum of the residents of all these census tracts. The total population served by each bank, in turn, is the sum of the residents of census tracts served by each of its individual banking offices.

correspondence between the local demographics of MDI office locations, the lending activities they undertake, and the communities they endeavor to serve. This section compares the demographic characteristics of service areas of MDI institutions with those of non-MDI community and noncommunity banks, and explores lending by these groups of institutions in the context of these demographic characteristics.

This evaluation of the social impact of MDIs is based on a unique estimate of the relevant *geographic service area* of each institution (see inset box above). The results show that compared with other financial institutions, MDI offices tend to be located in communities with a higher share of the population living in LMI census tracts and with higher shares of minority populations. In addition, MDIs originate a greater share of their mortgages to borrowers who live in LMI census tracts and to minority borrowers compared with community or noncommunity institutions.

### Comparing the Share of Population Living in LMI Tracts

Based on these computed geographic service areas, comparisons can be made of the populations served by MDIs with those served by non-MDI community and noncommunity banks. The first such comparison, undertaken for 2006 and 2011, indicates that the share of service area populations that live in LMI census tracts is higher for MDIs. In fact, the share of estimated service area populations living in LMI tracts was substantially higher for African American, Hispanic American, and Asian American MDIs, compared with both community banks and noncommunity banks (see Chart 5.1). For example, in 2011 the median non-MDI community bank operated in a service area in which 17 percent of the population resided in an LMI census tract. By comparison, the estimated service area population living in LMI tracts for the median African American MDI was 66.5 percent, or 3.9 times the share for the median non-MDI community bank. Similarly, the

Chart 5.1

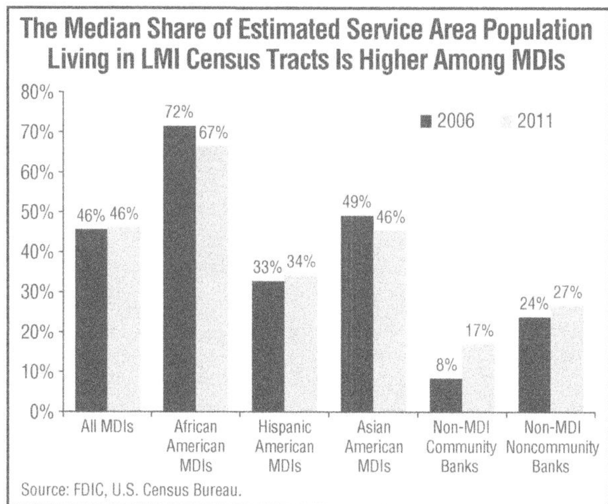


median Hispanic American MDI's estimated service area had 34.1 percent of its population living in LMI tracts, while the median Asian American MDI's estimated service area had 45.5 percent of its population living in LMI tracts.

## Estimated Service Area Minority Populations

Having offices in minority communities is also important to providing access to mainstream financial services. A 2011 FDIC survey showed that 10 million "unbanked" U.S. households did not have bank accounts with mainstream financial institutions, and another 14 million households could be considered "underbanked."[18] The survey also indicated that minority households were more likely than other households to be unbanked. Some 21.4 percent of African American households and 20.1 percent of Hispanic American households were found to be unbanked in 2011, compared with 4 percent of white households.

MDIs are important service providers to minority populations, which tend to have higher percentages of unbanked households than other population groups. Using the geographic service area designations, MDI offices are shown to be located in areas with a higher share of minority populations. Analysis of the demographic characteristics of these service areas reveals that in both 2006 and 2011, the minority share of estimated service area populations was much higher for all three groups of MDIs compared with non-MDIs. For example, in both 2006 and 2011 the median share of estimated

Chart 5.2

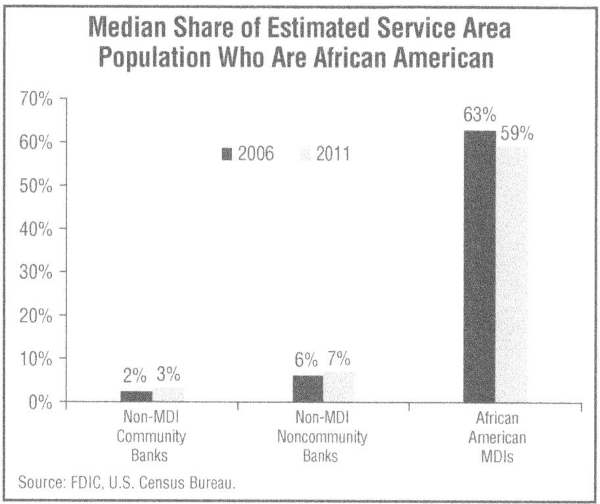


Chart 5.3

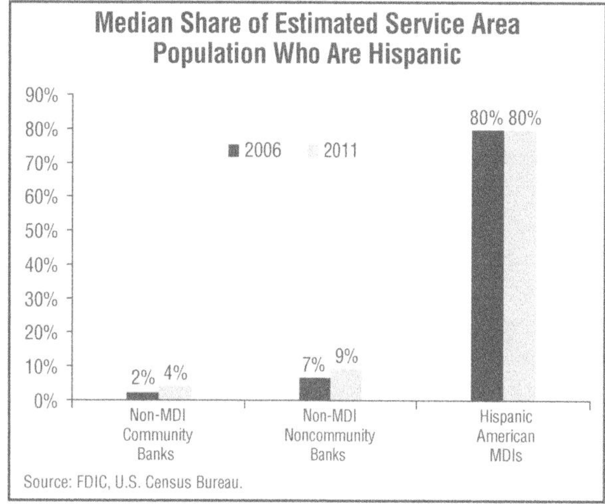


service area population who were African American was roughly 60 percent for African American MDIs, compared with less than 7 percent among community and noncommunity banks (see Chart 5.2).

Hispanic American MDIs have service area populations with an even higher median share of Hispanic American residents compared with non-MDIs (see Chart 5.3). In both 2006 and 2011, the median share of estimated service area population who were Hispanic American was nearly 80 percent among Hispanic American MDIs compared with roughly 9 percent or less among community and noncommunity banks.

Asian American MDIs also have service area populations with a higher share of Asian Americans compared with non-MDIs (see Chart 5.4).

[18] See *2011 FDIC National Survey of Unbanked and Underbanked Households*, http://www.fdic.gov/householdsurvey/.

Chart 5.4

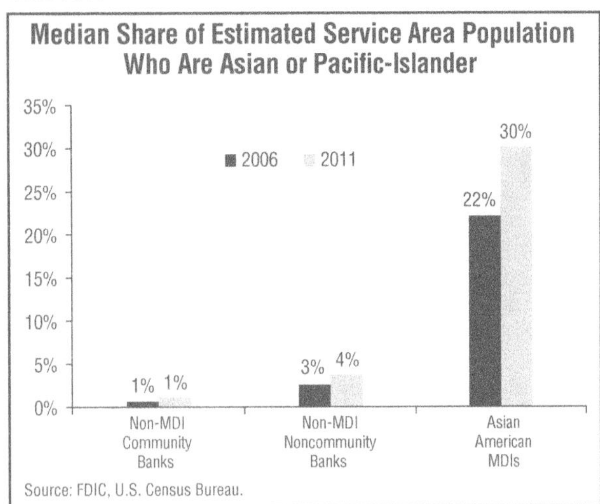


Chart 5.5

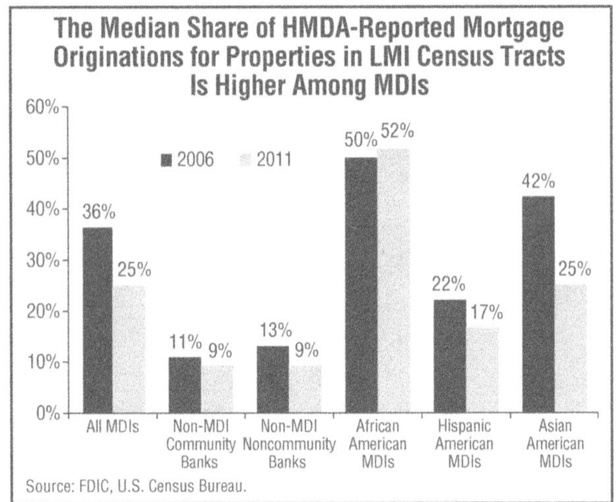


## Home Mortgage Lending of MDIs

MDIs not only maintain offices in communities with higher LMI population shares than other institutions, but among banks that report data under the Home Mortgage Disclosure Act (HMDA), MDIs also originate a greater share of their home mortgages to borrowers whose properties are located in LMI census tracts.[19, 20] For example, in 2006 the median African American MDI originated half of its HMDA-reportable mortgages to borrowers for purchasing properties in LMI census tracts (see Chart 5.5). This is more than 4.5 times the share of mortgages originated to such borrowers by non-MDI community banks and more than 3.8 times the share of mortgages originated to such borrowers by non-MDI noncommunity banks.

Chart 5.5 shows that between 2006 and 2011 the share of mortgages originated in LMI census tracts declined for every group of institutions except African American MDIs. Still, in 2011, the median shares of mortgage loans made on properties located in LMI census tracts by MDIs exceeded the share made by non-MDI community banks by anywhere from 2.6 to 5.5 times.

Chart 5.6

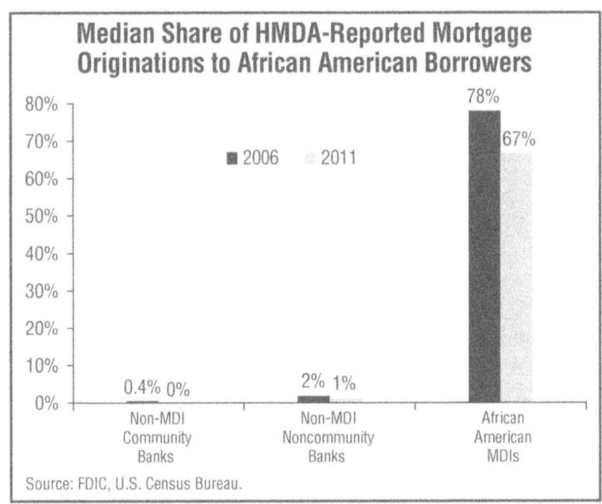


African American MDIs appear to be particularly successful in their mission of serving African American borrowers. Chart 5.6 shows that the median share of HMDA-reported mortgages made to African American borrowers in 2006 was 78 percent for African American MDIs, compared with less than 1 percent for non-MDI community banks. While the median share of mortgages made to African American borrowers fell to 66.7 percent for African American MDIs in 2011, it still far exceeded the less than 1 percent share reported by non-MDI community banks in that year. In fact, the share of mortgages made to African American borrowers by African American MDIs exceeded the already-high share of African Americans residing in their service area by 78 percent to 63 percent in 2006 and by 67 percent to 59 percent in 2011.

[19] Depository institutions that meet three criteria must report HMDA data: (a) assets as of December 31 of the year preceding data collection exceed an annually adjusted threshold ($40 million for collecting 2011 HMDA data and $35 million for collecting 2006 HMDA data); (b) on December 31 of the year preceding data collection, the institution had a home or branch office in an MSA; and (c) in the calendar year preceding HMDA data collection, the institution originated at least one home purchase or refinance loan secured by a first-lien on a one-to-four-family dwelling.

[20] HMDA reportable mortgages are home purchase, home improvement, and refinance mortgages. Home equity lines of credit for home purchase or improvement may be reported at the institution's option (FFIEC 2010).

Chart 5.7

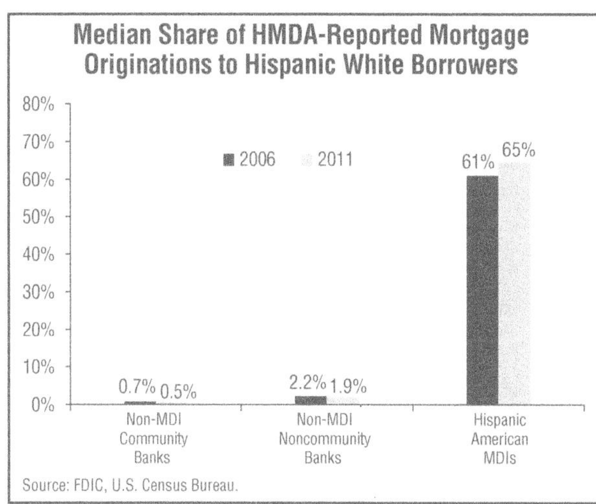


Chart 5.8

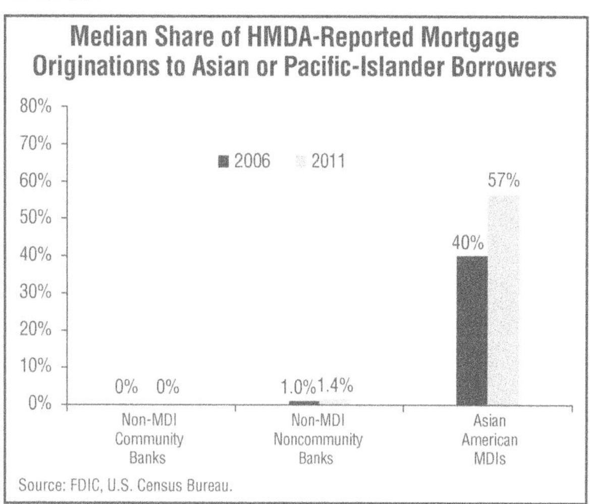


Hispanic American MDIs also appear to be highly successful in their mission of serving Hispanic American borrowers. Chart 5.7 shows that the median share of HMDA-reportable mortgages made to Hispanic American borrowers in 2006 was 61 percent for Hispanic American MDIs, compared with less than 1 percent for non-MDI community banks. In 2011, the median share of mortgages made to Hispanic American borrowers rose to 65 percent, while the share remained at less than 1 percent for non-MDI community banks.

Finally, Asian American MDIs also originated a higher percentage of their mortgages to Asian American borrowers. Chart 5.8 shows that the median Asian American MDI originated 40 percent of its HMDA-reportable mortgages to Asian American borrowers in 2006, compared with less than 1 percent for non-MDI community banks. By 2011, the median share of mortgages made to Asian Americans by Asian American MDIs had risen to 57 percent, while the median share for non-MDI community banks remained at less than 1 percent. Similar to African American MDIs, the share of HMDA-reported mortgages originated by Asian American MDIs in 2006 and 2011 exceeded the median shares of Asian American populations they served in both years (22.1 percent in 2006 and 30.1 percent in 2011, shown in Chart 5.4).

***Section Summary***

Compared with non-MDI community banks, MDI offices tend to be located in communities with a higher share of their population living in LMI census tracts and a higher share of minority residents. In addition, in a comparison of mortgage lending based on analysis of Home Mortgage Disclosure Act data, MDIs originated a greater share of their mortgages for properties located in LMI census tracts and to minority borrowers compared with non-MDI community and noncommunity banks. These group differences were quite substantial in magnitude and were found to be statistically significant using two different statistical tests. On the basis of these comparisons, MDIs appear to be highly successful in carrying out their mission of serving low- and moderate-income as well as minority households.

## Are There Statistically Significant Differences in the Demographic and Income Characteristics of the Geographic Service Areas of MDI and Non-MDI Community Banks?

Our comparison of the social impact of MDIs and non-MDI community banks has shown that MDIs serve higher percentages of populations residing in LMI census tracts and originate higher percentages of mortgages to LMI and minority populations. But are these differences statistically significant? To answer this question, we follow the techniques applied to comparisons of financial performance in Section 4 and conduct two statistical tests using the same observational techniques: the t-test and the Wilcoxon rank-sum test.

The t-test compares the distribution of the share of the estimated service population living in LMI census tracts and the share of HMDA-reported mortgage originations for properties in LMI census tracts, and tests whether or not the mean values reported for both groups are equal in a statistical sense. A Wilcoxon rank-sum test is also employed to indicate whether the overall distributions for the two subject groups differ to a statistically significant degree. Both tests were applied to the share of service-area populations residing in LMI census tracts and the share of HMDA-reportable loans made on properties located in LMI census tracts for 2006 and 2011 (see Chart below).

The t-tests and Wilcoxon rank-sum tests both consistently indicate that differences in population demographics and lending characteristics between MDIs and of non-MDI community banks are statistically significant. MDIs reported significantly higher shares of service populations living in LMI census tracts than did non-MDI community banks in both periods, and also reported significantly higher shares of HMDA-reported mortgage originations in LMI census tracts as well. From the results of our analysis, it appears that statistically meaningful differences exist between MDI and non-MDI community bank service area demographic and mortgage origination characteristics. Additional information related to these tests and the methodology is available in the Appendix.

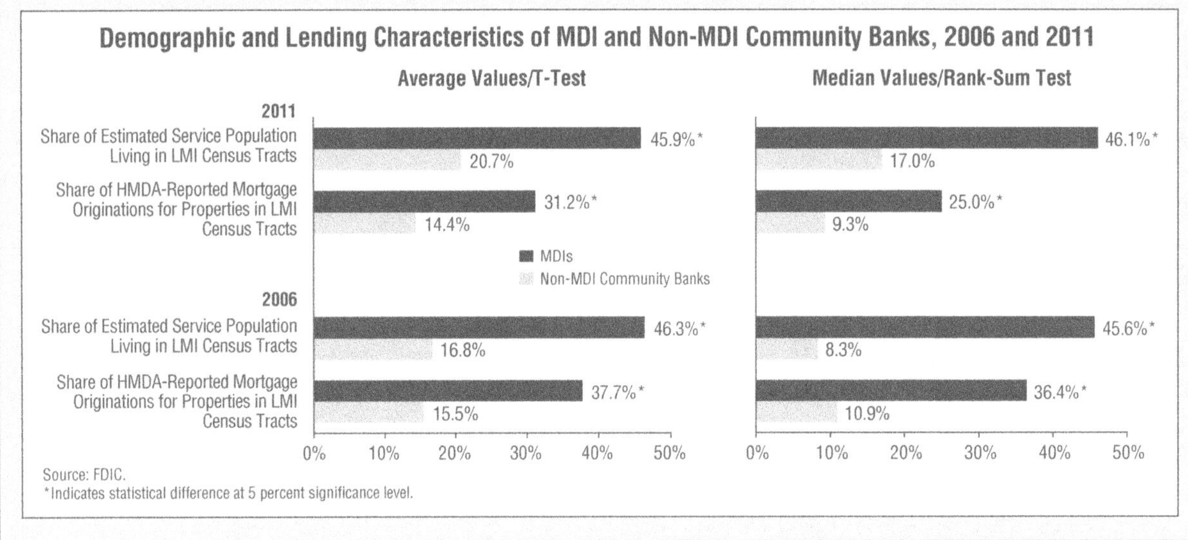



*Authors:* *Eric C. Breitenstein, Economic Analyst*
*Division of Insurance and Research*

*Karyen Chu, Chief*
*Division of Depositor and Consumer Protection*

*Kathy Kalser, Assistant Director*
*Division of Insurance and Research*

*Eric W. Robbins, Regional Manager*
*Division of Insurance and Research*



*The authors would like to thank Benjamin R. Backup, Camille Campanella, Andrew Driscoll, Denis Dudnik, Miguel Hasty, Cody Hyman, Schuyler Livingston, Alexander Marshall, John McGee, Arthur Micheli, Silvia L. Ramirez, Rachelle Rose, Dhruv Sharma, Ronald W. Sims II, and Benjamin Tikvina for their significant contributions to the analysis of MDIs undertaken in this study.*

## APPENDIX: Additional Information on the Statistical Significance Tests

### Data

We perform an observational study on FDIC-insured financial institutions that compares data on MDIs to data on non-MDI community banks. In an observational study, the assignment of subjects to groups is nonrandom and outside the control of the observer. Although our results indicate statistically significant differences exist between certain financial metrics of MDIs and non-MDI community banks, our results do not prove that being an MDI is the only reason for these differences. This is because of the possible existence of confounding factors. For example, MDIs may have greater exposure to poorer-performing markets than community banks in the aggregate. However, institutions in both subject groups operating within the same market may perform similarly. Further research into the comparative financial performance of MDIs and non-MDI community banks could compare institutions operating within the same geographic area to institutions located outside the area.

As noted earlier, the comparative analysis of financial performance of this study was completed in connection with the 2013 Interagency MDI/CDFI Bank Conference, and is therefore based on bank-level data from the December Call and Thrift Financial Reports each year from 2001 through 2012. These data are used to calculate the following financial ratios for each bank: pretax return on average assets, annualized net interest income, annualized noninterest income, annualized noninterest expense, annualized provisions, and the efficiency ratio. Each ratio is calculated by dividing the appropriate income statement item by an institution's five-quarter average assets.

A key assumption made in constructing some statistical tests is whether the variables of interest follow a *normal distribution*. As part of our analysis, we tested pooled and annual cross sections of the financial ratio data for normality using the Anderson-Darling, Cramer-von Mises, and Kolmogorov-Smirnov tests. In every case we rejected the null hypothesis of normally distributed population at significance levels less than or equal to 1 percent.

The data were also found to be heavily influenced by *outliers*, or observations well outside of a variable's usual range. For example, a handful of banks report efficiency ratios in excess of 10,000 percent, and two dozen report efficiency ratios greater than 5,000 percent. Similarly extreme values are also found among the other variables. To the extent that the goal of conducting statistical tests is to compare means or medians between groups of institutions, the presence of these extreme values can result in a misleading comparison. To minimize the influence of outliers, we limit our analysis to the core of observations that are within four standard deviations from the mean for all analysis variables. Any institution reporting a value greater than or equal to four standard deviations from the average for any analysis variable is defined as an outlier and is excluded from the analysis for that particular year. This process resulted in the exclusion of 1,926 of the 101,587 total observations available for the 2001–2012 period, or just fewer than 2 percent of all available observations.

### Statistical Tests—Financial Performance

In analyzing financial performance, we use a sample composed of annual bank financial performance metrics from 2001 through 2012. This sample is used to make inferences regarding the population distributions of MDI and non-MDI community bank financial ratios. For each analysis variable, we conduct statistical tests based on the null hypothesis that the population means or distributions are identical, and the alternative hypothesis that the mean or distribution for one population differs from that of the other population. For any particular comparison, our threshold for statistical significance is 5 percent. Comparisons that produce *p-values* smaller than 5 percent reflect statistically significant differences between the two samples. In many cases, the p-values we have calculated are less than 1 percent.

Our first comparison for each analysis variable was based on the *t-test*, which is commonly used to test whether the means of two samples randomly drawn from independent, normally distributed populations are statistically different. A *t-statistic* was calculated from the means, variances, and sizes of each subject group. Comparing this test statistic with values drawn from the Student t-distribution, we calculated p-values that express the probability that the null hypothesis (that the means are equal) is correct. Pooling all non-outlier observations for the 2001–2012 period, we obtained results for comparisons between MDIs and non-MDI community banks for six measures of financial performance.

As discussed previously, one caveat associated with these results is that the population distributions for each variable are likely not normal. Moreover, while observations made within any given year may be independent, observations for the same institution across years are unlikely to meet this assumption. To account for the lack of independence across years, these t-tests were also run for

Table A.1

| T-tests of Differences in Means of Selected Performance Measures of Minority Depository Institutions (MDI) and Non-MDI Community Banks, 2001–2012 | | | | | | | |
|---|---|---|---|---|---|---|---|
| | | Pretax ROA | Noninterest Income | Noninterest Expense | Net Interest Income | Provisions | Efficiency Ratio |
| Mean | MDI | 0.30 | 1.05 | 4.01 | 3.77 | 0.57 | 89.0 |
| | Non-MDI CB | 0.93 | 0.73 | 3.13 | 3.63 | 0.33 | 74.4 |
| T-test | t-statistic | 12.9 | -6.8 | -18.9 | -7.0 | -12.9 | -9.9 |
| | Interpretation | **MDI Lower** | **MDI Higher** | **MDI Higher** | **MDI Higher** | **MDI Higher** | **MDI Higher** |

Notes: The community bank is defined in the *FDIC Community Banking Study* (2012).
Variables other than Efficiency Ratio are expressed as a percent of average assets.
Reported averages are not weighted.
The t-statistic is a measure of the difference in means between two samples, adjusted by the sample sizes and variation of the data. Larger absolute values imply greater differences.
The significance level is the probability of observing the result by chance, so that lower values of the significance level indicate greater likelihood that the difference between the populations is not random. We consider the results statistically significant if the probability of observing them by chance is less than 5 percent.

each individual year. The signs of the relationships indicated in Table A.1 were observed in every individual year, while the p-values calculated for individual years were below 5 percent in all but a handful of cases. These results point to a consistent pattern of statistical relationships between group means as reflected in Table A.1.

Although the t-statistic is generally robust to moderate departures from the assumption of normally distributed populations, the fact that the populations are likely not normally distributed led us to conduct a second statistical test.[21] The Wilcoxon rank-sum test was proposed in 1945 by chemist Frank Wilcoxon as an alternative test for comparing two samples without the need to assume any particular form for their distributions.[22] Using this method, a test statistic is calculated based on the rankings of observations for each variable in the pooled sample. Within that pooled sample, the ranks for observations belonging to each sample are summed independently and scaled by the size of the overall sample. For samples for which the variable distributions are very similar, these scaled rank-sums will be nearly equal to one another. Alternatively, the sample distributions can be said to be statistically different if their scaled rank sums differ to a sufficient degree. This type of comparison can be used to test the null hypothesis of equal distributions for two populations (see Table A.2).

The results of the Wilcoxon rank-sum test in Table A.2 are perfectly consistent with the results of the t-test in Table A.1. This consistency of results adds to the robustness of our conclusion that the observed differences the financial performance between MDIs and non-MDI community banks are statistically significant.

## Statistical Test—Social Impact

A parallel set of statistical tests are applied below to the comparisons between MDIs and non-MDI community banks in terms of the social impact measures described in Section 5. Table A.3 applies a t-test to the comparison of mean values between these two groups for the share of service-area populations residing in LMI census tracts and the share of HMDA-reportable mortgages made on properties located in LMI census tracts. In both cases, the rather large differences in sample means observed in Section 5 are found to be statistically significant at the 5 percent level.

A parallel set of t-test results (not reported here) also indicates statistically significant differences in mean values for these social impact variables between MDIs and non-MDI noncommunity banks.

Because these comparisons of the mean values for social impact variables depend on the same statistical assumptions as the t-test applied above to financial performance variables, we also undertake a second statistical test based on the Wilcoxon rank-sum test. The results in Table A.4 indicate that, compared with non-MDI community banks, MDIs serve a significantly higher share of populations residing in LMI census tracts and originate a significantly higher share of HMDA-reportable mortgages in LMI census tracts. A parallel set of comparisons between MDIs and non-MDI noncommunity banks (not reported here) also indicates significantly higher shares for MDIs in terms of both measures.

[21] See Dennis D. Wackerly, William Mendenhall III, and Richard L. Scheaffer, *Mathematical Statistics with Applications*, 7th ed. (Belmont, CA: Brooks/Cole, 2008).

[22] See Frank Wilcoxon, "Individual Comparisons by Ranking Methods," *Biometrics Bulletin*, 1, no. 6 (Dec. 1945): 80–83, http://www.jstor.org/stable/3001968.

Table A.2

| Wilcoxon Rank-Sum Tests of Differences in Distributions of Selected Performance Measures of Minority Depository Institutions (MDI) and Non-MDI Community Banks, 2001–2012 | | | | | | | |
|---|---|---|---|---|---|---|---|
| | | **Pretax ROA** | **Noninterest Income** | **Noninterest Expense** | **Net Interest Income** | **Provisions** | **Efficiency Ratio** |
| Median | MDI | 0.7 | 0.71 | 3.62 | 3.78 | 0.28 | 77.0 |
| | Non-MDI CB | 1.14 | 0.58 | 2.96 | 3.62 | 0.17 | 68.4 |
| Rank-Sum Test | p-value | <0.01 | <0.01 | <0.01 | <0.01 | <0.01 | <0.01 |
| | Result | **MDI Lower** | **MDI Higher** | **MDI Higher** | **MDI Higher** | **MDI Higher** | **MDI Higher** |

Notes: The community bank is defined in the *FDIC Community Banking Study* (2012).

Variables other than Efficiency Ratio are expressed as a percent of average assets.

The significance level is the probability of observing the result by chance. Lower p-values indicate greater likelihood that the difference between the populations is not random. We consider the results statistically significant if the probability of observing them by chance is less than 5 percent.

Table A.3

| T-tests of Differences in Means of Selected Social Impact Measures of Minority Depository Institutions (MDI) and Non-MDI Community Banks | | | | |
|---|---|---|---|---|
| **Share of Estimated Service Population Living in LMI Census Tracts** | | | | |
| | | **2006** | **2011** | **Conclusion** |
| Mean | MDI | 46.3% | 45.9% | MDIs have higher shares of service area populations living in LMI census tracts |
| | Non-MDI CB | 16.8% | 20.7% | |
| T-test | t-statistic | 13.4 | 12.4 | |
| | Interpretation | **MDI Higher** | **MDI Higher** | |
| **Share of HMDA-Reported Mortgage Originations for Properties in LMI Census Tracts** | | | | |
| | | **2006** | **2011** | **Conclusion** |
| Mean | MDI | 37.7% | 31.2% | MDIs have higher shares of originations for properties in LMI census tracts |
| | Non-MDI CB | 15.5% | 14.4% | |
| T-test | t-statistic | 10.3 | 7.1 | |
| | Interpretation | **MDI Higher** | **MDI Higher** | |

Notes: The community bank is defined in the *FDIC Community Banking Study* (2012).

The t-statistic is a measure of the difference in means between two samples, adjusted by the sample sizes and variation of the data. Larger absolute values imply greater differences.

The significance level is the probability of observing the result by chance, so that lower values of the significance level indicate greater likelihood that the difference between the populations is not random. We consider the results statistically significant if the probability of observing them by chance is less than 5 percent.

Table A.4

| Wilcoxon Rank-Sum Tests of Differences in Distributions of Selected Social Impact Measures of Minority Depository Institutions (MDI) and Non-MDI Community Banks | | | | |
|---|---|---|---|---|
| **Share of Estimated Service Population Living in LMI Census Tracts** | | | | |
| | | **2006** | **2011** | **Conclusion** |
| Mean | MDI | 45.6% | 46.1% | MDIs have higher shares of service area populations living in LMI census tracts |
| | Non-MDI CB | 8.3% | 17.0% | |
| Rank-Sum Test | p-value | <0.01 | <0.01 | |
| | Result | **MDI Higher** | **MDI Higher** | |
| **Share of HMDA-Reported Mortgage Originations for Properties in LMI Census Tracts** | | | | |
| | | **2006** | **2011** | **Conclusion** |
| Mean | MDI | 36.4% | 25.0% | MDIs have higher shares of originations for properties in LMI census tracts |
| | Non-MDI CB | 10.9% | 9.3% | |
| Rank-Sum Test | p-value | <0.01 | <0.01 | |
| | Result | **MDI Higher** | **MDI Higher** | |

Notes: The community bank is defined in the *FDIC Community Banking Study* (2012).

The significance level is the probability of observing the result by chance, so that lower values of the significance level indicate greater likelihood that the difference between the populations is not random. We consider the results statistically significant if the probability of observing them by chance is less than 5 percent.

www.ingramcontent.com/pod-product-compliance
Lightning Source LLC
Chambersburg PA
CBHW080625180526
45168CB00007B/3057

* 9 7 8 1 5 1 1 4 2 9 9 1 7 *